Are You Sure You Are Ready To Be A Wife?

Fannie A. Pierce

Rapier

PUBLISHING COMPANY

Are You Sure You Are Ready to Be a Wife?
ISBN 978-0-9839483-0-8

Published by
Rapier Publishing Company
3417 Rainbow Parkway
Rainbow City, Alabama 35906

www.rapierpublishing.com
Facebook: www.rapierpublishing@gmail.com
Twitter: rapierpublishing@rapierpub

Printed in the United States of America

Book Design by: Drew Key (Key Koncept)/ Delaney-Designs

Book Layout by: Delaney-Designs

Dedication

I dedicate this book to my nieces: Nia, Tynisha, Jamilya, Sierra, Brandi, Brooke, Bianca, Shaye, Ashleigh, Miya, Taylor, Aubri, Darrian Christina, Bella, Savannah, Skhye Chappelle and the ones yet to be born. As you prepare or go through the journey of holy matrimony, I pray that when asked the question, "*Are you sure you are ready to be a wife?*" you can answer the question with honesty and assurance.

Love You,
Aunt Fannie

Special Thanks To

Majestic Dance Ministry,
Comanche Chapel, Fort Hood, Texas & Greater Vision
Community Church, Killeen, Texas

Daughters of Excellence (DOE),
United Christian Church, Gadsden, Alabama

To My Four Best "Special" Friends,
Neasell, Adrian, Avis & Syreeta
You were beautiful brides, now you're beautiful wives.

Thank you all for the opportunity to impart spiritual
wisdom into your lives.
I thank God for the privilege and grace to have such
wonderful spiritual daughters.

Thanks to my Awesome Editing Team:
Ms. Tiffinay Scott-King
Ms. Linda Lyle
Ms. Taiisha Walton
Ms. Jaime Evans

A Special Thanks to Angela Thornton
My Editing "Guru"

Table of Contents

Introduction

A couple of years ago, we heard the news that my beautiful spiritual daughter was about to journey down the road of holy matrimony. The thought of her getting married made me start thinking about what it meant to be a wife. Even though I knew she was ready, I still wanted to ask her the following questions: "Are you sure he's the one?" "Do you see yourself spending the rest of your life with this person?" And most importantly, "Did God send him to you?" I wasn't being skeptical, or the bearer of bad news. I knew she loved the Lord, and it was clear her fiancé was a godly man who loved her very much. So, this wasn't the case.

But as much as I wanted to ask her, I didn't. I couldn't. In her eyes, she saw stars and fireworks. She was glowing from the concept of being married; therefore, I didn't dare to tell her the other side of marriage that the bridal books don't talk about, or as we married folks say, the reality of marriage. You see, marriage is a wonderful institution designed and established by God, bringing two imperfect vessels together as one. And that's the reality of marriage, two imperfect people, coming together, committed, and dedicated to each other and the marriage, to fulfill a specific purpose. It sounds beautiful (and it is), but it's also self-sacrificing and sometimes extremely challenging.

I have been married to my husband for twenty years, and after all of these years, he still "rocks my world." He is still the sparkle in my eyes. However, I wouldn't be honest if I said that throughout the years everything was perfect. It wasn't. In fact, there were times I wanted to escape. Not get a divorce, but run away. I wanted to take a break or a vacation from marriage because sometimes it was too hard.

Being a wife is more than being a bride. It's more than waking up to your husband every day, cooking, cleaning, doing the laundry, etc. Once you get married, or begin to prepare for marriage, you have to come to the realization that how you used to live (or what you used to do) will no longer be your reality. Other than the Lord, your husband or husband-to-be will have a prominent place in your life. He will become a priority that you have never considered. His dreams, goals, and desires intertwined with yours will determine the success and outcome of your marriage. If you allow the Lord to lead and guide you in "how to be a wife" to your husband, the outcome will be victorious for the both of you—pushing you into your destiny. However, if you resist or rebel against the grain or the leading and guiding of the Holy Spirit, your marriage might result in failure.

For the first ten years of my marriage, I didn't understand the true calling of a wife. I didn't understand my role, responsibility, or purpose as a wife to my husband. I went against the grain and this cost me setbacks, failures, and precious time that I can't get back. That's why I am writing this book, guided by the Holy Spirit. I am allowing you to see my errors, so that you will be better prepared as a wife.

I pray as you read this book that you allow the Lord (through the guidance of the Holy Spirit) to minister to you on what the Bible says about a wife. By the way, this is not a book on how to be a wife. Instead, this is a book that provides you with understanding and a biblical foundation on the application or the assignment of a wife.

Whether you are about to be married, or one day hope to get married, may you be blessed and enlightened as you embark on this journey into holy matrimony. And when asked the question, "Are you sure you're ready to be a wife?" you can answer the question with both honesty and confidence, "Yes, I am."

If you are reading this, and you are married, you can now possibly answer the question with, "I may not have been ready, but I am now."

God Bless

Chapter One

The Humor in Prince Charming and Cinderella

"Who can find a virtuous woman? for her price is far above rubies..." Proverbs 31:10 (KJV)

When we are preparing for our wedding, we don't realize that it's only a day. A very special day, but still, it's only a day. However, being a wife is more than a day. It's a lifetime commitment, or as my husband says, "You are a bride for a day, but a wife for life." Sadly, many of us get wrapped up in the day. We focus on the bride and the wedding. Here come the bride, all dressed in white. Everyone looks glamorous, and everything is perfect. And why not? It's the bride's day, and on this day, it's all about the bride. It's pretty poignant how we plan for the day, but never the marriage.

At every wedding I've attended with my husband, I've cried. He doesn't. But, he does get sentimental when he sees me crying. I cry because the bride is a picture of beauty and elegance, walking down the aisle, looking starry-eyed at her prince charming. I look around, and the majority of the women are crying too. Our outside tears portray the emotion of the event, yet our insides are singing a different tune. We dare not tell her the real deal, or what she is getting into. We will keep that to ourselves because for the moment, it's her day, and we let her have her day. Although, we do tell her after the fact, but over a period of time, and in small portions, when she learns that being a bride is nothing like being a wife.

Unfortunately, on the wedding day, even troubled marriages appear normal. For a brief moment everything is going to be okay. However, the reality is that when you get home from the wedding, you are not the bride and groom. You are husband and wife, and sometimes it's not going to be okay. I guess that's why we allow the bride to have her day, believing her prince has come to sweep her off her feet as they do in the fairy tales. The funny thing about fairy tales is, they are just fairy tales. Your husband wasn't looking for a bride or a princess. He was looking for a wife, or as I say jokingly to Pete, he was looking for a maid. I don't intend to come off as condescending- just a little humorous, because in marriage, you will need it.

The bridal books and magazines will not tell you about the days after the wedding. They are not going to inform you on how to handle a crisis when it comes: when your husband loses his job, when you are barely speaking to each other, and worse, when you can't stand the sight of each other. They are not going to tell you that there may be times that you will want to leave, you will think about a divorce, or worse get a divorce. The books and magazines won't tell you that there will be moments you long to be single again, when it was only you, and not another person to think about, when you could go and do as you pleased. They will not tell you about the tragedies, the heartaches, and the turbulence that can destroy even the best of marriages. No, their job is to sell the bride, not the wife.

Now looking back, it's funny that neither of my marriages depicted the wedding I planned in my youth nor what the bridal books portrayed. With my first marriage, I eloped and got married at the courthouse. I wore a pink dress that I had in my closet, and he wore his military dress blue uniform. We had to hail a cab to the courthouse. My oldest sister was the only witness. After the clerk pronounced us husband and wife, we went back to my apartment so I could pack my bags for school. The next day, I was heading off to Fort Huachuca, Arizona to attend a six-month Officer's Basic Course (OBC). Three years later we were divorced.

For my second marriage, I did get married in a church. The wedding took place in Baltimore, my home town. We had to plan the wedding from Texas, where we both were stationed at the time. I left all the arrangements with my sisters. I gave them what I'd perceived was plenty of time to prepare for a wedding-four months.

We were getting married in the fall, so I selected fall colors for my wedding. My bridesmaid's dresses were emerald green, and the groomsmen wore black tuxedoes with black bow ties. Even though I was married before, I wore a white gown. (It was as if I was a virgin again with Pete. God gave me a new beginning.) Pete wore a white tuxedo. He looked very handsome.

Well, the first thing that didn't go as I had planned was the bridesmaid's dresses. When I got into town and went to the seamstress, the dresses were not finished even though she'd had plenty of time (can we say bridezilla?). That's when I noticed the design of the dresses was changed, and my sisters were the culprits. It didn't matter if they thought the new design looked better; they changed the design. I had my reasons for the design.

When I addressed them about it, they ignored me. I was hoping my mother, who was also at the fitting, would take my side, but she didn't. She took their side. The earrings were the next change. I wanted small, dainty earrings. They wanted big—not flashy earrings, but big enough to see. So, although I paid for the earrings, my little sister, who was also my maid of honor, wore big earrings. Yes, she looked beautiful, but they weren't what I'd selected.

It gets better! At the end of the rehearsal dinner party, tensions were high and my eldest sister and I got into a heated discussion. The next day, which was my wedding day, with a tear-stained face, I went to the hair dresser, who was a friend of both of ours. There we were at the hairdresser together but not speaking to each other. On my way out of the salon, still upset with my sister, I saw a guy driving a limousine. Luckily, he got stopped at the red light and I was able to track him down by foot and give him my sister's home address and told him to be there at a specific time. I didn't know if he would show up, but God was with me. At 4 p.m. promptly, the limousine driver was there at the door waiting for us. He didn't recognize me at first because that morning when he saw me, my face was tear-stained and I looked rough due to lack of sleep.

My wedding coordinator, who was my sister's friend, hired a singer with a deep voice that I didn't care for. He probably would've been okay, if he had selected a song better-suited for his baritone voice. It sounded as if karaoke had invaded my wedding. If it wasn't for my sister-in-law being an anointed singer who graciously sang, I don't know what I would have done. Not to be undone, the piano player came in looking as if he had stepped out of bed. He put on a robe to cover up his messy attire. It wouldn't have been bad if it wasn't for the fact that he had on dirty tennis shoes. You could see them when he sat down because the piano was in full view. The photographer was the icing on the cake. He took a lot of pictures; however, at the reception, he had to borrow money to get home. And worse, when he came to show us the pictures, he informed us that he had forgotten to put the film in the camera. Of course, we didn't pay him the balance, but at that point I didn't care. Thankfully, my husband's friend had taken a lot of pictures and we used those, and they were free.

I failed to mention that I lost my voice before the wedding ceremony. You could barely hear me when I said my vows. My father-in-law said I looked as if I were ready to run during the entire ceremony. I looked afraid—maybe not afraid, but I knew what he meant. Overall, in spite of everything, and I mean everything, the wedding was beautiful. As I walked down the aisle and saw my handsome husband to be, who looked as if he was going to devour me, I knew I made the right choice. You see, he was ready for a wife, and I was ready to be his wife.

Oh yes, the reception! If you think the photographer was the icing on the cake, the reception was the cherry on top. When we arrived into Baltimore, I discovered that I didn't have a place reserved for the reception. I didn't even know if we were going to have a reception. You guessed it! I had to make the arrangements. I had to book the reception hall, order the food, and get a music coordinator (DJ), all because the person responsible for reserving a place forgot to make the arrangements. There I was, two days before my wedding, 7 p.m. in the evening meeting with someone I just met about my reception. (He was a friend of a relative.) I didn't know what to expect when I walked into the reception, but again, God took care of everything. The reception hall was decorated beautifully, and the food was delicious. (By the way, the reception went well. My sister and I made up.)

When it was time to leave the reception, we said our good-byes and thanked everyone for coming. Before we went to the hotel, we stopped by my sister's home to look at the gifts, and ended up staying longer than planned. It was late when we finally arrived at the hotel and I was tired. I didn't want to do anything but sleep. However, sleep was not on my husband's mind.

No, the bridal books don't tell you all of things that will happen before, during, and after the wedding. They tell you what you want to hear, or believe. Again, their job is to sell the bride. Where were the reality shows back then, because I was definitely a candidate? Where were the people who had told me that my wedding day was going to be the happiest and least stressful day in my life? Where were those who had told me that I was going to be the princess for the day? They didn't tell me the truth! They wanted me to buy into the fantasy. The myth of Cinderella, Snow White, Sleeping Beauty, and all the other animated cartoon heroines who longed for their Prince Charming to come and sweep them off of their feet. My prince didn't sweep me off my feet; instead, he gave me a broom (metaphorically speaking). He didn't need a fairy tale princess. He needed a wife.

And that is what I am to him. I'm not his bride. I am his wife. As a wife, I don't necessarily enjoy the struggles, the downs, the setbacks or tribulations, but they come with the territory. Yet, I do like how adversity brings us closer together in the end, depending on each other, but more importantly depending on God to bring us through. This makes us more focused on the marriage, and more focused on Him; our Lord. I like how sometimes my husband can get me so upset that I want to hit him, but at the same time he can melt my anger away by saying, "I'm sorry," or giving me a peck on my lips. I like it when we both finish each other's sentences, how we laugh together, cry together, hold each other, and even after all these years still love each other. I like it when I have to learn how to submit to him. It's teaching me how to be the woman God needs me to be for him.

No, marriage is not a fairy tale; it's real, with real people who are different, but come together to do what God ordained them to do. It's not for the weak of heart, because sometimes, more often than we want to admit, it's downright hard. And if we don't understand the foundational structure and principles behind marriage, we can get lost in the fairy tale. For you see, you may be looking for a Prince Charming, but your husband or fiancée is not looking for a Cinderella. He is looking for a wife.

In regard to Cinderella, I don't think I could be her. Life would be boring without challenges, because let's face it, marriage is challenging. By the way, have you ever noticed that the animated cartoons never show you what happens after the Prince comes, finds his bride, and they ride into the sunset looking lovingly at one another? I wonder what Cinderella found waiting at her door when she rode up to the castle?

Chapter Two

When a Man Finds a Wife

"Whoso findeth a wife findeth a good thing, and obtaineth favour of the Lord." Proverbs 18:22 (KJV)

Marriage is a covenant between God, the husband and the wife. God said it's not good for man to be alone, so He made man a wife (help meet). Therefore, when a man takes a woman to be his wife, he is entering into a holy covenant before the Lord God Almighty. He is saying to the Lord, while surrounded by family and friends, that he takes this woman to be his wife.

The woman in the covenant is saying to family and friends, but more importantly to God, that she agrees to be this man's wife. She agrees to be the wife the man needs to complete his assignment in Christ. She agrees to leave her single status and become one with the man. Selflessly she doesn't think of herself; she joins forces with her husband, and the two become one in their ways and desires to please the Lord. Her talents and gifts are to enhance and complete the man. They are to make up for his inabilities; hence, we get help meet. When the man knows this is the type of woman he has married, he knows he has found a good thing.

The NLT version of Proverbs 18:22 reads, *"The man who finds a wife finds a treasure and receives favor from the Lord."* I like this translation. It tells me how a good wife is both a treasure and a blessing to her husband and how the Lord is pleased with her, bestowing favor to the man for having found her.

In order to find a treasure, you have to dig and search for it. Rarely would a hidden treasure be on the surface for someone to stumble upon it. All valuable treasures are buried deep beneath the earth's surface, in hopes of never being found. There may be replicas found, but the true treasure is buried very deeply. Only a rare few, who really want the treasure, go to the extra lengths to find it. Many of us want the goods or the *"booty"* of the treasure, but not what it takes to retrieve it. This is the same way with a *"good"* wife. We want to be wives, but we don't want to be hidden in God for the man to find us. We want the accolades of being a wife, but not the true treasure of what the Lord says about being a wife. We don't realize that when a wife is hidden, waiting to be found, she can properly bring her treasure to the marriage.

I know a lot of you are saying, "This is the twenty-first century, and we don't believe in this type of nonsense!" You are right, and that is why you don't have a husband. You don't want to be found. You want to be the one who finds the man. Ouch! The truth hurts. Regardless of what century we are in, God's ways and Word are still valid and true. The man finds the wife, not the other way around. Don't believe the hype, or the world's view on statistics of men- women ratio, even the statistics that proclaim many men, (especially African-American men) are in prison; therefore, the odds of women getting married decreases with age. The devil is a liar. Those are the world's statistics, not God's. The Lord doesn't operate this way.

I know Christian women who have been married on more than one occasion. I am one. For whatever reason, the death of a spouse or a divorce, they're still found by a man. In God's Kingdom, there isn't a man shortage. If there is a delay, it may be because you may not be ready to be found. The Lord, in His infinite wisdom and love for us, wants the best for us. After all, He gave His best, His only begotten-son Jesus Christ:

"For God so loved the world, that he gave his only begotten Son, that whosoever believeth in him should not perish, but have everlasting life." John 3:16 (KJV)

Since He gave of His best, don't you believe He wants the best for us in every aspect of our lives, including marriage? Marriage is difficult enough because you have two people from different backgrounds, cultures, mannerisms, and beliefs (not religions, because I believe that believers shouldn't be unequally yoked with nonbelievers. That's the Word!). If the Lord doesn't settle for less, it seems right to say, He doesn't want you to either. Yes, the man is everything you want, but he's not saved. This may not be God's best for you. Wait until God saves him before you marry Him. I've seen too many women marry men who tell them that they are Christians, or they will get saved after the marriage, only to find out after the vows they're not saved, and weren't planning on getting saved after the marriage. They said those things to get these women to say yes.

Now, not to put you in bondage, because every marriage is not set up this way, there are instances when you marry an unsaved man, and because of your walk, he gets saved. There is also the scenario where two unsaved people get married and within the course of the marriage, they receive salvation. There is grace for every marital setting. However, when you know in your "knowing," and God is showing the warning signs or the red flags, don't settle for less. Wait for God to send you His best. His best is His Word. I've been on both sides and His way is much better.

When you go out and find a man, you are not going to see in him what God sees in Him. Many women are emotional when they go on the "hunt" for a man. Why? Because we are women. We see the surface; we see the now. God not only sees the now, He sees the future. He sees the end result. He knows what's in store for you if you choose your own husband. He sees the unnecessary trials and tribulations, the heartaches, the disappointments, and the failures which were not part of the original process or path He had ordained for you. However, since you chose your husband, this is the path you have to go down. Yes, sure, it's still good, but ask yourself, "If this is good, how much better would it have been if I'd allowed the Lord to select my husband?" What could have happened if I'd allowed myself to be hidden in Christ until my husband found me?" There are many women today who regret their decisions because they didn't wait on the Lord.

Also, waiting on the Lord doesn't mean living together as if you are married. You are not husband and wife. You are a man and a woman living together, playing house. You want the blessing of the marriage covenant, but you don't want to abide by the covenant stipulations. That's like saying you want a paycheck for work you didn't do. You can't expect the marriage blessings if you are not in a covenant marriage. When God sends you your husband, he is not going to cause you to sin, nor take you away from your relationship with the Lord. He is supposed to enhance it, not hinder it.

I know what you are saying or thinking; but, before you close the book, hear me out. For too long we have accepted sin because we were afraid of being offensive. While we are being politically correct, the world (which includes our loved ones) is dying both physically and emotionally because of sinful lifestyles. I know that we all have, and still do sin; however, as a believer, if you find yourself continually sinning without regard or respect for God and His Holy Word, you better check yourself. No man, no matter how fine or prosperous he is, should cause you to sin, or to stray away from your relationship with Jesus. If he wants to have sex with you, he should put a ring on your finger. This is why I reiterate, when the Lord hides you, He is not going to let anyone find you. The man who finds you will be a blessing and not a curse.

I'm not judging you. This is the word of God. The Lord states throughout the Bible to stay away from sexual sin. In Exodus 20:14 (KJV), one of the Ten Commandments is, *"Thou shalt not commit adultery."* If this wasn't important to the Lord, why did He make it a commandment? No, we are not under the Law anymore; we are under grace. We are saved by grace through faith in Jesus Christ. Grace doesn't keep you sinning. Grace turns you away from sin because it is directional.

For the majority, the Lord does want you to have a husband. I say majority because there are women God has ordained to be single. This gift comes from the Lord. The women who have this gift have accepted this call and are at peace with God about His course for their lives. For the ones who do not have this calling, the Lord does want you to have a husband, but He knows that many of you are not ready to be wives. He wants to hide you for a while to prepare you, so when you are found, you can bring your treasures to the marriage. Believe me, there is a difference between you being found and you finding someone. How do I know? I am a living witness. I chose my first husband.

On the surface, he was everything I wanted in a man. He was intelligent, handsome, professional, and came from a well-to-do family. In my mind, and in the minds of on-lookers, we were a successful, upcoming, professional couple, who appeared to have it all together. We didn't. All we had was a glass house waiting to be shattered. And after three years, it did. Looking back, I realize I was caught up in the fairy tale of riding off into the sunset with Prince Charming. There wasn't a sunset; it was just an illusion. The illusion I had, like so many women, is that if I had a husband, if I was only married, I would be complete. What an illusion.

My divorce, although painful and very detrimental, did have a marvelous outcome. Because of it, I repented and went back to my Father, who was waiting with open arms to receive me. However, because of the hurt and heartache from the divorce, I had made up in my mind that I was never going to get married again. I was going to stay in the presence of the Lord. He was going to be my husband. Those were my plans, but the Lord had other plans for me. During the course of my healing, the Lord hid me. I was hidden in Christ, and while in my hidden state, I became content with being single.

That was the key. I was not looking for a man. I was content, happy, and peaceful being in the presence of the Lord, learning about His ways and His Word. I had a successful career, beautiful home, and money in the bank. What more could I have asked for? Because I was focusing all of my attention in Him and on Him, He was working some things out in me. The

Lord was preparing me to be found. He started working on my surface issues of insecurity, pride, and the arrogance of being a successful, professional woman. (My in-depth issues were another matter. They took some time.) Unbeknownst to me, I was in training to become a wife.

While I was being hidden, I wasn't worried about being held or caressed by a man. My God was holding me and caressing me. When I got frightened at night from being alone in the house, He was there to protect and keep me. When I became lonely, He was there to comfort and talk to me. Why did I need a husband when I had the Lord? I was hidden in Him, and as a result, He was building up my treasure chest. I didn't even know that I was in the process until after my husband came to find me. That's how it is when you are hidden in Christ. You won't know until you are found.

This is where Jesus wants you to be. He wants your mind and heart on Him, trusting in Him, not looking for a husband. He wants you sitting at His Feet. Why should He allow you to be found when you rarely sit at His feet now? Once you're married, other than a crisis or a trial, He would not hear from you. I know women who were sold out for Jesus, yet once they got married, their husband became the center of their universe. Remember, God is first, *"Thou shalt have no other gods before me,"* Exodus 20:3 (KJV). If you are putting your husband before the Lord, he has become your God. You are idolizing him. Why should the Lord give you a husband if it is going to keep you in idolatry?

You see, the Lord knew I was ready to be found because I wasn't interested in a husband. My focus was on and in Him. He knew I would keep Him first because I kept saying I didn't want a husband. In fact, I told the Lord that if I were to get married, He would have to choose my husband. I chose the first one and look where it got me – a lot of pain.

Now, while I was being hidden, Pete was searching for a wife. He had a couple of serious relationships, including an engagement to one woman. In his process of looking for a wife, he told the Lord the type of woman he was searching for, and I fit the category. (Sounds as if it's a meat market, but it's not. It's really beautiful and spiritual, after all, I didn't know he was also having this type of conversation with the Lord.) God was working everything out for our good.

I will never forget the day I met my husband. It was at a gospel concert. I didn't want to attend, but my friend who purchased the tickets persuaded me to go. I'm glad I did. The moment I saw my husband, I knew there was something about him. It wasn't love at first sight; it was a spiritual connection. He felt the same way too. How do I know? He told me. He was praying and looking for a wife.

He searched high and low, and found some replicas of a wife, but they were not the real thing. The Lord showed him in his quest where to find me. I was the hidden treasure the Lord had buried for my husband. As a result, my husband found me because I was ready to be found. We met June 3, 1993, got engaged three weeks later, and got married 4 ½ months later on October 16, 1993. I never looked back. Has it always been easy? From the outside it appears that it has, but it hasn't been. The difference between my marriages is that my first one was built in a glass house; my second was built on the foundation of God. God ordained it because I was a treasure waiting to be found. I was a good thing.

Chapter Three

Waiting To Be Found

"[1] Abraham was now an old man, and the Lord had blessed him in every way. [2] One day Abraham said to the man in charge of his household, who was his oldest servant, [3] "Swear by the Lord, the God of heaven and earth, that you will not let my son marry one of these local Canaanite women. [4] Go instead to my homeland, to my relatives, and find a wife there for my son Isaac."
Genesis 24:1-4 (NLT)

In Genesis Chapter 24, Abraham, stricken with age and about to die, asked his trusted servant to go into the land of his family and find his son, Isaac, a wife. Even in his old age, Abraham knew he didn't want his son to marry a woman of the world. He wanted his son to be married to a woman with the same background he had. Today, we call them believers.

Abraham's servant wanted to take Isaac with him, but Abraham told him no. He told his servant that the Lord would send an angel ahead of him to find a wife for his son. The servant obediently went to his master's homeland to find a wife for his son. While in his search, he asked the Lord a specific request pertaining to the woman who was to be found. He asked that she would offer him a drink of water for himself and his camels. The Lord heard his request for a wife for his master and honored it:

"[15] As he was still praying, a young woman named Rebekah arrived with a water jug on her shoulder. Her father was Bethuel, who was the son of Abraham's brother Nahor and his wife, Milcah. [16] Now Rebekah was beautiful, and she was a virgin; no man had ever slept with her. She went down to the spring, filled her jug, and came up again. [17] Running over to her, the servant asked, "Please give me a drink." [18] "Certainly, sir," she said, and she quickly lowered the jug for him to drink. [19] When he had finished, she said, "I'll draw water for your camels, too, until they have had enough!" [20] So she quickly emptied the jug into the watering trough and ran down to the well again. She kept carrying water to the camels until they had finished drinking. [21] The servant watched her in silence, wondering whether or not she was the one the Lord intended him to meet. [22] Then at last, when the camels had finished drinking, he gave her a gold ring for her nose and two large gold bracelets for her wrists." Genesis 24:15-25 (NLT)

When Rebekah gave the servant a drink, he immediately knew she was the one to be found. She was a kinsman of his master, Abraham. With this revelation, he began to praise the Lord for answering his prayer.

"[26] The man fell down to the ground and worshiped the Lord. [27] "Praise be to the Lord, the God of my master, Abraham," he said. "The Lord has been so kind and faithful to Abraham, for he has led me straight to my master's relatives." Genesis 24:26-27 (NLT)

After meeting with her family and making all of the arrangements, the servant was ready to depart and return to his master, Abraham. He inquired if he could take Rebekah with him. Rebekah's family wanted her to stay with them for an additional ten days. The servant persistently stated that he wished to return to his master as soon as possible, so they asked Rebekah what she wanted to do. Rebekah's response was that she wanted to go with the servant to his master and his master's son, Isaac, her future husband. She didn't want to wait; she was ready to be found. As Rebekah was about to depart, saying her last good-byes, her family blessed her with a blessing that was a treasure for her husband:

"Our sister, may you become the mother of many millions!
May your descendants overcome all their enemies."
Genesis 24:60 (KJV)

When they reached their destination, Rebekah looked and saw her betrothed watching as they approached. When Isaac went to meet them, Rebekah dismounted the camel and covered her face with her veil. The servant told Isaac the story of how he was sent out by Abraham to find a wife for him. When Isaac heard the story, he took Rebekah into his deceased mother's tent, and she became his wife. Isaac loved her very much. She was a special comfort to him after the death of his mother, Sarah.

In the previous chapter, we spoke about the man who finds a wife finds a good thing. She is not only a good thing; she is also a treasure for her husband. Her husband is blessed and highly favored with both men and God because of her. I'm not being redundant. I want you to see with your spiritual eyes what I am trying to convey to you. Rebekah didn't know that she was being hidden. She didn't know that one day at the well, while she was taking care of her Father's business, He was going to bless her with a husband. She didn't know that giving a stranger a drink of water would change her destiny forever. Rebekah was in a waiting period. She didn't know it until the day she was found.

How can I make such a statement? Easily. The moment she saw Isaac, she connected with him spiritually, not sexually as we often times do. At once, she started respecting and reverencing him by dismounting the camel and covering her face with her veil. They went into his mother's tent and consummated the marriage. She provided him with the comfort he needed to get over the death of his mother, Sarah. She was what he needed, and she also had what he needed.

Rebekak was at the well. In this day and time that would be equivalent to her being at her place of employment, or working on a project. She was busy with her task; not wasting her time daydreaming about a man. She wasn't idle, or hanging out with the "*girls*" gossiping, complaining, or up to no good. She was about her Father's business. She was assigned by her family to carry water to and from the well. That was her job, and she did it in an exemplary manner. How do I know this? Because she was the one who was found.

When Pete came and found me, as with Rebekah, I knew he was the one. No one had to tell me because the Lord was preparing me to be his wife. In my waiting, I went about my day-to- day business. No, I wasn't perfect, but I did have a great time in my single period. I went to movies and dinners with friends, and many times I did those things alone. I enjoyed being by myself. I didn't need anyone to tell me how special I was. The Lord told me. I wasn't idle with the girls, gossiping, complaining, or wishing I had a man. I was at my well taking care of business. (The well is not a physical place, per se; symbolically speaking, it is a place of being hidden in Christ.)

As far as sex, when I got divorced, I prayed to the Lord to take away my sexual desires. Was I perfect? No. Did I stray sometimes? Yes, on rare occasions; but, I always repented and turned back. I wasn't happy with the outcome of backsliding; however, my backsliding didn't stem from wanting or needing a man. It came from the emotional perspective of being divorced. I felt abandoned and rejected. In those rare times, I felt that I had to prove to myself that I was a desirable woman. Thank God for deliverance because even though it happened on very few occasions, wrong is wrong. If I continued on that path, without allowing the Lord to heal me in my brokenness, I would not have been found by Pete. I would've had men coming in and going out of my life, but that would have been it. The Lord was not going to give me one of His best when I was a mess.

Let me reiterate, the man who finds a wife finds a good thing. I don't care what you want to believe, morals and values are still important. As my grandfather would say, "Why buy the cow, when you can get the milk free?" A man who is looking for a wife is not going to look in the places where everyone else is looking. He doesn't go to the familiar places or scenes. No, he digs and digs until he finds the treasure he's been searching and praying for. Now, I am not against the club scenes, or bars; however, having spent enough time in both in my early years, I can say without hesitation, rarely is a man looking for a wife in these places.

When a man is searching in a club, he is looking for a woman. There is a difference. The wife does him good and provides him favor. The woman may give him temporary pleasure, but not what he needs. I am not saying you can't meet your future husband at a club or bar, but if you are looking for a man there, you may be looking in the wrong places. If you happen to be hanging out and having fun with the girls and you meet a man looking for a wife, that's different. However, having grown up in the city, with brothers and plenty of male friends, I know that the majority of times men are not looking for a wife when they visit those places.

In regard to waiting to be found, don't think the stories of Isaac and Rebekah, Jacob and Rachel (Genesis 29), or even Joseph and Mary (The Gospels) are a coincidence. All of those men were looking for a wife. The wives were hidden. When it was time, they were found, and not before the appointed time. You can go out on your own and find a husband, but is it according to the word of God? And, more pertinent, if you are impatient in your waiting on the Lord to prepare you, you may marry the wrong man. Sometimes this is worse than not having a man. As I previously stated, there are many women who wish they could take back their *"I Do,"* but they can't. They made a covenant with the Lord. When the minister says, *"For better or for worse,"* they are living the worse. (If you are in this type of marriage, praise God. He can make all the crooked things straight).

Also, when a man comes claiming you as his wife, you should have a peace about it; it should be confirmed in your spirit by the Holy Spirit. This is no joke. I dated a couple of men who really liked me. One guy did ask me to marry him. (He and I only went out a few times. I thought that we were just friends, but he wanted more). What these men saw was a woman who loved the Lord, and was about her Father's business. She wasn't idle, but hardworking, diligent, industrious and uncompromising. I was what they wanted, or perceived, in a wife. Yet, when they demonstrated an interest in me, I knew they were not the one. How did I know? I was hidden in Christ.

One gentleman was God-fearing, attractive, and he owned a successful business. Many women would've jumped at the chance because he was well-off and handsome. On the surface, he had it going on, but for someone else, not me. I knew he wasn't the one, for two reasons. My spirit confirmed he wasn't, and he had two precious young daughters. I wasn't ready to be an instant mother. I wasn't prepared to raise another person's children. Another incident I encountered was when a guy told me I was his wife. He was serious. Again, if I wasn't hidden in Christ, I would've married the wrong man.

When you are ready to be found, you'll be found, and not before the appointed time. The turkey may look brown on the outside, but it's still undone on the inside. Enjoy your single life. This is where God has you, for now. It may feel like it's taking an eternity, but wait on the Lord. Don't go before your time. Don't rush the process. Don't become impatient. After all, you don't want to marry the wrong man.

By the way, don't let others persuade you to marry the wrong man. Don't allow anyone to make one of the most important decisions in your life for you. If you are not sure, or don't have a peace, the majority of times this means that it's not the Lord. God is not the author of confusion, *1 Corinthians 14:33*. I don't care if they think you make a cute couple, or if they believe he is the one for you. Cuteness only goes so far. Even if your parents or friends are saying he is the one, you better get a confirmation in your spirit man, after all, they don't have to live with him until death do you part. If it is of God, believe me, God will get you together in His timing. I know some faithful God-fearing Christian women who listened to significant others and married the wrong man. Now they have to live with this secret and regret.

I knew Pete was my husband. It was confirmed by significant others, including my mother; however, it was first confirmed in my spirit. I always tell people, your heart knows the real answer. Listen to it. That's where the Spirit is. The Holy Spirit will never lead you wrong.

Chapter Four

He Is Your Ministry

"Parents can provide their sons with an inheritance of houses and wealth, but only the Lord can give an understanding wife."
Proverbs 19:14 (NLT)

As a wife, your husband is your ministry. After the Lord, your husband should be your second priority, not the children, your career, or your college degree. I know this sounds absurd, especially since we are in the twenty-first century, and it's all about "Girl Power." (One thing about "Girl Power," and that is it has no power if it's not connected to the Holy Ghost power). I know what I'm saying sounds as if I'm taking women back to the Stone Age. You know the picture when the caveman hits his wife over the head with a club, while dragging her into the cave. Well, I'm not referring to this depiction; I am coming from the Word of God.

Always know the Lord is a God of order and structure. His Word never changes. We change, but He doesn't. Heaven and Earth will change but His Word will not, *"Heaven and earth shall pass away, but my words shall not pass away,"* Matthew 24:35. Whether you want to debate this or not, God's Word is Truth. And according to His word, there is order and structure. When we don't have order, we have confusion, and the Lord is not into confusion. *" For God is not the author of confusion, but of peace, as in all churches of the saints,"* 1st Corinthians 14:33.

You may think I am crazy now, but if you keep reading, I promise you will begin to understand the meaning behind these words, (and not through my words, but through God's Holy Word). That's why I always ask women who think they are ready to take the step into Holy matrimony, "Are you sure?" or "Did the Lord tell you to do this?" Again, I'm not trying to second guess them or be spiritual. They must know that this is a serious step and a life-time decision. When a woman is about to be married, she must know who she is and she must have done all she wanted to do as a single female before she says, "I do." The minute you say, "I do," it's no longer about you. It's about God and the marriage. That's why you need to pray to the Lord when the man asks you to marry him. You better inquire of the Lord, not only about whether he is the one, but also if you are ready to be a wife.

I recently finished writing my book, *"Helpmeet Or Hindrance: Which One Are You?"* This was where I was. I was a good wife; however, in some major areas in the marriage I was a hindrance. The sad part about it was I didn't know I was a hindrance in these areas until the Lord revealed it to me. You couldn't tell me I wasn't a good wife to my husband. I perceived I had it "going on." But, I didn't. And nine times out of ten, you don't either. You think you know everything there is to know about being a wife. You think you know all the answers as they relate to being a wife. You listen to all the talk shows portraying powerful women, because after all, they appear to have all the answers for women. I have news for you, many of them are not married, and they may never get married. I am not knocking them. I say bravo to them, if this is the choice they have made. I remember my grandmother telling me when I was seeking marital advice from a single woman, she said, *"Honey, why are you taking advice from a single woman when she doesn't have a man?"* Wow, thank God for her wisdom! I still use this advice today.

Before I continue, I need to tell you about myself so you will understand that I am not preaching to the choir; I am also talking about me, who is also in the choir. Before the Lord delivered me, I was classified as a type "A" personality. I was very independent and wanted to be in control. I didn't want to depend on a man for anything. Even though I was a woman, in my subconscious mind, I became a man. This stemmed from my father leaving us when I was ten years old. As a result of him not being there, my mother had to struggle to pay the rent and buy us food. When my father was there, due to his addiction to alcohol (which eventually killed him at the early age of forty-six), he rarely brought home his paycheck. I kept all of this concealed in my young mind.

I made peace with my father when I was nineteen. I didn't want to become bitter or hindered as an adult. I told him on his deathbed that I loved him and forgave him for abandoning us. However, unbeknownst to me, subconsciously his absence from my childhood did have an impact on me that I carried over into my adult life. Seeing my mother struggle and go without, made me not want to trust a man. No man was going to control me.

Committed, focused and strong-willed, I was determined to be someone and have nice things. After high school, I joined the Army Reserves. After excelling in this task, I decided to attend college. In college, I joined the Army Reserves Officers Training Corps (R.O.T.C.) to become an officer in the United States Army. In college, I excelled both in my academics and R.O.T.C, winning many prestigious awards and citations. I was President of the Political Science Club, Battalion Commander for R.O.T.C, Student Government Officer, Who's Who Among Colleges and Universities, National Dean's List were just a few of my accomplishments.

It was also in college where I met my first husband. After graduation and being commissioned in the army as a Second Lieutenant we got married. He was also an officer. Finally, my life was on the right track, or so I thought. With my pace, positive attitude, and love for the military, I was determined to do twenty years and obtain the rank of a full bird Colonel. I was focused, and nothing was going to stop me. Not even God. Oh, I was saved, but it was all about me and my plans.

Things didn't go as I had planned. You know the story. We got a divorce after three years of marriage. I repented and went back to my First Love, the Lord. However, even after returning to the Lord, I couldn't forget the pain and hurt from the divorce. I couldn't forget the shame and humiliation. I was determined not to let a man have that much control or power over me again. I didn't say it vocally, but in my mind, I did. Unfortunately, I took this mindset into my second marriage. I built strong walls that it took the Lord years to penetrate because, although I loved Him, I didn't want to get hurt again. The Lord has a great sense of humor. Everything I said I would never do, I did. No, not in the beginning, it took years and believe me, it was a long and painful process. Why? Because I fought, kicked, screamed, and cried all during the process.

My flesh was learning how to submit to the Lord and His will for my life, and it didn't like it. During the tenure of the marriage and fighting against the will of God, I got out of the military, and not because I wanted to; it was best for the marriage. I lost my job. We moved to an unfamiliar land. In this new, unfamiliar land, I couldn't find employment. When I did start working, I was almost terminated. During this process, I quit my job, got rehired, quit again and started working for my husband. In addition to the pain of all of this, my excellent credit, which I prided myself on, went from an A+ to an F. Eventually, I had to file bankruptcy. My pride, dignity, and all of the things that I considered important were stripped from me. I became unsure, insecure, and lost, all because I wouldn't obey the Lord and be a wife (help meet) to my husband (who, at the time, didn't know any of this was happening).

I wanted my will and my way. I wanted to have my cake and eat it too. After all, I baked it. What I failed to comprehend was that when I said, "I do," my plans were no longer the priority. The marriage took precedence and my plans now took the back seat. Everything I wanted to do, I should have done when I was single. I know it sounds as if I'm one-sided, but I'm not. The husband has a major role in the marriage too. He has to answer to God for whatever he does or does not do pertaining to his wife and family. That's why I continue to reiterate that you better make sure he is the one for you. By the way, although your initial plans have to take a back seat, they will happen. Not in your timing, but according to God's appointed time.

You see, I had to learn that Pete was not only my husband, he was also my ministry. How he treated me, was not the issue in the Lord's eyes. It was how I treated my husband when he wasn't acting like my husband. I would always say to the Lord, *"Lord you are being unfair. Don't you see what Pete is doing? Don't you care how he is acting?"*

It appeared that God was taking sides, and I was always on the wrong side. During the process, I believed that the Lord didn't care about me, or what I was going through. To me, Pete was his favorite. When I became frustrated or anxious, He would inform me that He wasn't concerned with what Pete was doing at the moment. He would take care of Pete. He was focusing on me. For five years, the words that He spoke to me were, *"If you take care of my business, I will take care of your business."* The Lord knew where I was going and what I was created to do. I didn't. I didn't understand the process of becoming a wife. I didn't want to be purged or go through the fire. But I had to, and you do too.

During the process of submitting my will to His, the Lord showed me that Pete and his uniqueness was my ministry. The Lord was looking at how I treated the man He sent me. After God, Pete had to become my second priority. I literally had to learn how to love my husband the way Jesus loved me. Here I was an imperfect vessel, who Christ Jesus sacrificed Himself and died for in order for me to live. This was the way the Lord wanted me to love my husband.

So, for a season, I had to sacrifice my life, my dreams, my goals, my desires, and die to my will. I wanted to have a successful career in the military, and eventually become a lawyer and then a local politician. But the Lord's plans were different from mine. When I married Pete, my individual plans and dreams were put on the back burner. Notice I said, "My dreams." You see, I had to learn that it was no longer about me. Now it was about our dreams, intertwined with the assignment the Lord had for us to complete as a married couple. My destiny changed the moment I said, "I do." I became Pete's help meet, and he became my ministry.

How you minister to your husband is between you and the Lord. Yes, your husband has a role, but how you are to minister is based upon how the Lords shows and tells you. No two people are alike. You shouldn't base your entire perception of how to minister to your husband on another woman's perspective. That woman is married to another man, not your husband. Her husband's demeanor, mannerisms, and makeup are different than your husband's. They can only be used as examples. You should instead inquire about how to treat your husband from the One who created him, and that is the Lord.

My husband doesn't need for me to cook every day. Yours may want this from you. Don't base the needs of my husband on what you should do for your husband. Pete is my husband. I am his wife. I know his likes and dislikes. I know what makes him tick, what gets him upset, and what makes him laugh. I am not trying to minister to him based on how I see other women treat their husbands. Don't allow anyone to put you in bondage regarding the way you should treat your husband based on their perception, or ideals. True, men are the same in many ways, but they are also different in many complex areas. The complexities are based upon culture, ethnicity, family background, upbringing, belief systems, and their individual perceptions.

Also, don't worry if he is not learning things about you. Allow God to take care of that facet. You concern yourself with ministering to him. This pleases the Lord. Is it frustrating at times? Yes! Remember, I cried, fought, kicked and screamed during the entire process. It was hard. But, regardless of how hard, I had to go through it, because it never was about me. It was, and still is, about the Lord. My rewards will come from God, not man, and not my husband.

How do you minister to your husband? Be his wife. Be what he needs. I am not just talking about sex. Sex does play a significant part in the marriage, but it's not the most important aspect. Society has glamorized it to the point that even Christians perceive great sex as the key to a successful marriage. It is a key, but rarely does it open the door. If all you have is great sex and no foundation, that's all you have. Sooner or later your marriage will come up short, and perhaps fail because you based it on sex. Furthermore, cooking, cleaning, and keeping a neat house don't constitute a great and successful marriage either. As women, we've heard through the years that the way to a man's heart is through his stomach. This is not true. Cooking and cleaning are important, but again, they won't open the door.

A wife can be a blessing to her husband by encouraging him, being available to him (again, not just sex), and praying for him. (Pray continually and without ceasing for him). These are the greatest gifts a wife can give her husband. You should be your husband's biggest fan and cheerleader. There are many things Pete can do; yet, there are quite a few things he attempts to do, but can't. Sometimes he causes the situation to get worse. For example, when he attempts to fix the plumbing, and other mechanical things around the house. I always support him.

Even when I am calling the plumber or electrician to fix his mess, I support him. I always tell him I believe in him and that he can do all things through Christ, who strengthens him. If I don't believe in him, or cheer for him, who will?

Sometimes I have to be his nurturer, his pick-me-upper, and his encourager. On a few occasions, some of the decisions he made were detrimental to our family. Instead of complaining, or saying, "I told you so," (which, in the back of my mind I wanted to do), I comforted him and let him know that regardless of what was done, I was with him. I had his back. I was his wife. (Now, I wasn't always here. This was a process too, which I'll discuss in upcoming chapters.)

There are times when I have to minister to him with the Word of God. Other times, I have to lay hands on him when he is going through, or if he's under attack in his body from the enemy. I am the woman God sent to Pete. I have to be what God needs me to be for Pete. I have to minister to him because he is my ministry. How can I minister to others effectively if I can't minister to the one God sent to me?

Chapter Five

Your Husband Needs What You Have

"And the Lord God said, It is not good that the man should be alone; I will make him an help meet for him." Genesis 2:18 (KJV)

"[21] And the Lord God caused a deep sleep to fall upon Adam and he slept: and he took one of his ribs, and closed up the flesh instead thereof; [22] And the rib, which the Lord God had taken from man, made he a woman, and brought her unto the man. [23] And Adam said, This is now bone of my bones, and flesh of my flesh: she shall be called Woman, because she was taken out of Man."
Genesis 2:21-23 (KJV)

Many married women will tell you that although they thank God for their marriage, marriage is a lot harder than they imagined it would be. Their Prince Charming wasn't a prince after all, but an imperfect vessel who required a lot of attention and needed a great deal of help. He didn't ride off with her on a white horse into the sunset, taking her away from her problems. What he did was bring her to a place with many issues and problems, hoping she could help fix or manage them. Again, while you are looking at him as your Prince Charming, he is looking at you as his wife. Someone who will cook, clean, manage, nurture and help him. He didn't say this while he was courting you. He knew better. If he had, you would've run away. While he was courting you, he was bestowing you with words of sweet nothings in your ears, showering you with flowers, candy and gifts, while professing his undying love for you. He was hoping you wouldn't catch on to how he was smoothing you over to be his wife, not a fairy tale princess.

I can recall when Pete was courting me, he told me that he would always wash my car and make sure I had gas in the tank. He said I would never have to do these two things. Though his words were very sweet, I knew he couldn't fulfill his promises. He didn't. He did try, but after two months into the marriage he stopped. Funny thing was, he didn't have to woo me with campaign promises, I knew he was the one. I did inquire about this to him one day, and you know what he told me? He said, "I told you those things to get you." Did I get mad? No. As I said, I knew they were sweet, heartfelt, yet, meaningless words. They were campaign promises. Beautifully spoken, yet unfulfilled actions.

When a man is looking for a wife, he is looking for someone he is compatible with. Someone who fits into his God-given plans, even if he doesn't know them in the beginning. For this reason, he seeks God for his wife. He tells the Lord what he desires in a wife. The Lord, being the good Father that He is, gives the man not always what he asks for, but what he needs.

A husband needs a wife to help him accomplish his assignment from God. He needs a help meet to assist him, not hinder, manipulate, or control him. He doesn't need a princess. He needs a queen. A princess is still in training. A queen is ready to reign with her king. She is taught to sacrifice herself and her desires for the sake of the kingdom, which is the assignment of the king. When she takes her rightful place, she and her king rule together. She has the entire kingdom at her feet. That is the role of a wife: to assist him with his assignment. God gave man (Adam) his purpose before Eve was created. We can't say this happened after the fall, for the scripture tells us:

"[26] And God said, Let us make man in our image, after our likeness: and let them have dominion over the fish of the sea, and over the fowl of the air, and over the cattle, and over all the earth, and over every creeping thing that creepeth upon the earth. [27] So God created man in his own image, in the image of God created he him; male and female created he them. [28] And God blessed them, and God said unto them, Be fruitful, and multiply, and replenish the earth, and subdue it: and have dominion over the fish of the sea, and over the fowl of the air, and over every living thing that moveth upon the earth." Genesis 1:26-28 (KJV).

Adam's assignment or purpose from the Lord was to be fruitful and multiply, and replenish the earth, subdue, and have dominion over it. The Lord knew Adam was not capable of fulfilling this by himself. He wasn't equipped for this. Therefore, the Lord said it wasn't good for man to be alone; he needed a help meet. He needed someone to assist him in getting the task done. Thus, the Lord made woman and gave her to man. When Adam saw Eve, he knew she was what he needed to complete the assignment. He called her bone of his bones and flesh of his flesh. He called her *"Woman"* because she came out of him. Eve was always in Adam; but, she had to wait until she was needed to be manifested in the natural.

As with Eve, you have what your husband needs. You don't come into the picture until he is ready for a wife, and then the manifestation comes into fruition. Many wives, or soon to be wives, believe that their husband is supposed to provide them with their desires, goals, and purpose. And they do...if we are assisting them with their purpose. If a man doesn't become complete, or fulfill his assignment, you may never complete or fulfill your purpose in the marriage. The man needs you, because you have what he needs. That's why he went looking for you. If he already had it, he wouldn't have searched for you.

This is a hard pill to swallow for many of today's women, but it comes from the Word of God. I am not saying that the Lord doesn't want women to be doctors, lawyers, CEOs or even presidents. What I am trying to convey is that there will be times when you will have to take a backseat with your plans, and help your husband complete his assignment first. Oh, by the way, as a wife, your dreams and goals should intertwine with that of your husband. There cannot be two visions in the house. (We will discuss this in the next chapter).

I never realized the role or responsibility I had as a wife to my husband until I received this revelation. As I stated before, my goals were to be a colonel in the army, a lawyer and one day a local politician. Yes, I was a wife, but those were my goals. I didn't care about my husband fulfilling his assignment because I was too busy focusing on me. I didn't know I was hindering my husband by trying to kick against the curb and do my own thing, until the Lord showed me how I was headed for destruction. On the outside, I appeared to have it together; but, internally, I was a spiritual mess. I was out of order. I failed to grasp that if he didn't complete his assignment, the marriage would not reach its full potential. Pete needed me. That's why he went out to find me.

My strengths in organization, administration, and structure were what he needed. He was not as strong in those areas as I was. The areas where he was strong, I was weak. When we got married, his strengths became my strengths, and my strengths became his strengths. Together, we were strong enough to complete the task. Pete has start up ability. I have finishing ability. Pete has the vision. I have the fortitude to get the vision accomplished.

As women, every day, unless we are our own bosses, we go out and make others successful and wealthy. We give our all to our jobs, our bosses, and our assigned tasks. We stay up all night to finish projects, and work long hours to get the praise or the promotion. We give our God-given abilities, strengths and gifts to everyone else so they can complete their assignments. However, we tend to complain, grumble, and sometimes despise the one who needs it because he is not what we expected him to be as a husband. Yes, he may be a couch potato, a lazy slob, or maybe he watches sports all day and night, but he was the one you wanted. Remember, when the minister asked you, "Do you take this man?" you said, "I do."

Your husband may be an unkind, mean-spirited person, and you are the complete opposite. You can either complain or despise your husband for this, or you can give him what you have to help him overcome his unpleasant disposition. You can give him your gifts, while praying for God to change him. Love him as the husband you see in the spirit, and not the one you see in the flesh. If you give up on him, you'll never know his full potential. The Lord knew what type of man your husband was before you married him. He knew he was temperamental, unaffectionate and moody. In all of this, the Lord knew that you had what this man needed to help him complete his assignment. Don't complain, help him.

Pete needed what I had. When I shifted the focus from myself to him and gave him my treasures and gifts, he began to flourish into the man God needed him to be. He began to be more about the Lord's business. I couldn't concentrate or focus on if he didn't appreciate what I did, or gave up for him, which he does, but again, I couldn't focus on this. When I became his wife, I relinquished my former life. Not me per se, but my will and my selfish desires. (He still needs my personality, laughter and craziness.) When I want to cry because the sacrificial labor of love of giving up everything hurts, I know that I don't have to understand or get the big picture, because the Lord sees everything. To me, one of the hardest jobs is to be a God-fearing Christian wife. Why? You may never see the results of your sacrifice until you meet Jesus.

When Adam saw Eve for the first time, he knew she was to be his help meet. He knew in order for him to complete his assignment, he needed her special gifts as a woman. No one could help him achieve this but Eve. His assignment, even after the fall, didn't change- although it did come with detrimental consequences; it was still the same: *"Be fruitful, and multiply, and replenish the earth, and subdue it: and have dominion over the fish of the sea, and over the fowl of the air, and over every living thing that moveth upon the earth,"* Genesis 1:28 (KJV). Adam knew why he needed a wife. He understood her purpose. Adam, not God, called her Eve. *"And Adam called his wife's name Eve; because she was the mother of all living,"* Genesis 3:20 (KJV).

Final thought: Adam called his wife Eve because of her purpose. My questions to you are: Does your husband call you by your purpose? Does he have what he needs from you to fulfill his purpose?

Chapter Six

Vision vs. Purpose

"[22] Wives, submit yourselves unto your own husbands, as unto the Lord. [23] For the husband is the head of the wife, even as Christ is the head of the church: and he is the savior of the body. [24] Therefore as the church is subject unto Christ, so let the wives be to their own husbands in everything." Ephesians 5:22-24 (KJV)

"Wives, submit yourselves unto your own husbands, as it is fit in the Lord." Colossians 3:18 (KJV)

Of all the chapters I had to write, this was the hardest. If you don't read and understand this chapter in its spiritual context, it will lead to bondage. I'm serious. If not digested properly, you may believe that these words give men the upper hand to dominate and control women.

I cringe at the thought of immature *"want to be"* spiritual men getting hold of this without really understanding the contents, and putting their wives into bondage. Unfortunately, there are men who read the Bible without spiritual understanding and Godly wisdom. They base what they've read on their personal interpretation, making their wives' lives a living hell on earth. They fail to grasp what the Word of God intends when it says,

"Wives fit into your husband's plans." On the other hand, women who are in unfulfilled marriages will think that I am out of mind, or worse, I'm in a cult. They believe that my life must be a perfectly sweet cupcake, with pretty icing, and a cherry on top. It's not, nor has it ever been.

I believe one of the reasons we are challenged in the area of fitting into our husbands' plans is because religion has made it a burdensome task, resulting in many married women in bondage. Thus, once they become free, they vow never to go back to that way of life again. I have news for you! Anything that puts you into bondage is not from the Lord. Also, religion is man-made, with man-made rules and regulations. God's Word instructs us in this manner: *"God is a Spirit: and they that worship him must worship him in spirit and in truth,"* John 4:24 (KJV). Know that God's truth will make you free. *"And ye shall know the truth, and the truth shall make you free,"* John 8:32 (KJV). God's Word makes you free. It will never put you into bondage.

We spoke about this in chapters three and four; however, as it relates to this chapter, lets dig deeper. Before Eve was created, Adam existed. In Genesis 1:26-28 (KJV), it says, *"[26] And God said, Let us make man in our image, after our likeness: and let them have dominion over the fish of the sea, and over the fowl of the air, and over the cattle, and over all the earth, and over every creeping thing that creepeth upon the earth. [27] So God created man in his own image, in the image of God created he him; male and female created he them. [28] And God blessed them, and God said unto them, Be fruitful, and multiply, and replenish the earth, and subdue it: and have dominion over the fish of the sea, and over the fowl of the air, and over every living thing that moveth upon the earth."*

There are two major areas I want to concentrate on: (1) God established order, and (2) He made the man first. In order for a job, corporation, business, or administration to exist and function properly, there has to be an order. A structure or foundation without order will result in chaos and confusion, which will eventually lead to its destruction and demise. Someone has to be in charge. This is why we have a president, a boss, or a supervisor. Too many chiefs and not enough Indians will lead to defeat. The family is structured in this manner too. In God's plan, man is the head. He is the leader. This doesn't mean he is superior to woman. The Lord simply needed someone to be the head; and, because God is sovereign, He chose the male.

Before Eve was ever formed out of man; before she thought about eating the fruit, God gave Adam the vision for earth. It was to be fruitful and multiply, and replenish the earth. Even though the Lord created Eve to assist or help, Adam was the one responsible for the assignment, not Eve. When they fell, the Lord didn't go to Eve. He went to the one He gave the assignment to, or for better clarification, the vision to. He went to Adam.

"[8] And they heard the voice of the Lord God walking in the garden in the cool of the day: and Adam and his wife hid themselves from the presence of the Lord God amongst the trees of the garden. [9] And the Lord God called unto Adam, and said unto him, Where art thou? [10] And he said, I heard thy voice in the garden, and I was afraid, because I was naked; and I hid myself. [11] And he said, Who told thee that thou wast naked? Hast thou eaten of the tree, whereof I commanded thee that thou shouldest not eat?"
Genesis 3:8-11 (KJV)

As with Adam, the husband is the one responsible for the vision of the household, which includes the overall structure and operation of the house. As with a boss, the husband has an assistant, the wife. Whether the wife works or not, her role is not to be in charge, but to assist the one who is in charge. She is responsible for the day-to-day management of the home. Thus, the success or failure of the marriage is the man's responsibility; despite who is to blame. If there is a problem, he is responsible for dealing with it and getting it resolved. And, if there is a break in the foundation, because the Lord is a God of order, He is going to go to the man first to inquire about what happened, as He did with Adam.

God has given your husband a vision to complete while he is on this earth. You are to assist him. If he doesn't complete it, God is going to go to him, not you. This is somewhat hard to comprehend, let alone submit to, especially if your fiancée is not a leader, or this goes against everything you've been taught to believe since you were young. I can relate because this was how I felt. I was taught to be independent, and never to depend on a man. My divorce only intensified my beliefs, or strong convictions. Regardless of how I felt or believed, it was wrong. I was out of order. If you are not allowing your husband to take the role of the head in the marriage, then you are too. *And*, know by doing so, you are hurting him in the long run.

Please understand, God's Word does not imply that you don't have a vision. It means that you have to submit to the order of God for the marriage. God gave Adam the vision. When He created Eve, He gave Eve a purpose. Eve's purpose was to assist Adam with the vision.

You see, in the marriage, the husband casts the vision. The wife does have a Godly vision, but in the marriage, she humbly sets aside her vision and submits to the vision of her husband. There cannot be two visions for the marriage. A house divided cannot stand. *"And Jesus knew their thoughts, and said unto them, Every kingdom divided against itself is brought to desolation; and every city or house divided against itself shall not stand,"* Matthew 12:25 KJV. If both the husband and the wife have visions from the Lord for the marriage, there is confusion within the marriage. The marriage will not be successful if each one is trying to accomplish their individual vision.

Again, I am not implying that you can't be a doctor, lawyer, or CEO. What I am conveying is that whatever you do as a wife, it should fit into the overall vision of the marriage. Be mindful, if it is not benefiting the marriage, there is a possibility that you are doing your own thing. If you wanted to do your own thing, you should have stayed single. Before you say, "I do," ask yourself, "Am I willing to assist my husband in the vision? Do my plans and dreams fit into the overall vision of the marriage?" And finally, "Will the marriage be successful with what I am currently doing?"

I have a problem with women in ministry who say that the Lord gave them a vision outside of the one He gave to their husbands. I am not judging them for saying this. I can't. However, what they are saying appears to be outside of the order of God. When I read the scriptures, nowhere do I see a woman usurping the responsibilities of her husband. Remember, Jesus stated that a house divided cannot stand. If the Lord knew a house divided would not stand, why would He give two visions in the same household? Innocent people are getting hurt because we fail to adhere to the Truth. If you feel this strongly about the vision God gave you, don't ask, beg or cry to God for a husband. You don't want a husband. You still want to be in charge. Until you want to fit into another man's plan, you are not ready for

God's covenant called marriage. You want the convenience of having a man, without the sacrifice of being a wife.

If you believed that God has given you a vision, and the more you pray about it, the more He reveals it to you; you still have to wait on the Lord to reveal it your husband. You cannot go out before your appointed time. I know, because this was my case. I knew what God called me to do, but I had to wait until the Lord revealed it to my husband. It took ten years, but it was worth the process. When He reveals it to your husband, it will fit into the overall vision of the marriage. Always remember, God is a God of order. If we go out before the appointed time, we can abort the assignment and possibly the marriage.

To reiterate, as a wife, even though I am not given the responsibility of the vision, I do have something just as vital. I have a purpose in the marriage. My purpose is significant for the vision to be manifested. My husband needs me to complete his assignment. That is my purpose. As a wife, the vision needs your purpose to fulfill, or complete it. In Jeremiah 1:5 (KJV) it says, *"Before I formed thee in the belly I knew thee;"* and in Jeremiah 29:11(NLT), *"For I know the plans I have for you, says the Lord. They are plans for good and not for disaster, to give you a future and a hope."* These scriptures depict Jesus' plans for you. My purpose coincides with the vision the Lord gave Pete. My purpose in God fits into Pete's plans. Pete is called to be a minister of the Gospel. In being called to be his wife, I am assisting him in what God has called him to do, thus, fulfilling my calling too.

What I once perceived as important, to be a lawyer and politician, was no match for what the Lord had planned for my life, and that is to be a wife to my husband. When I submitted to His plans, God birthed (out of my obedience) my purpose. I am doing what I was put on this earth to do, fulfilling my calling in the Lord. If I had kept my plans, I don't know where I would be today. Probably like many women today, successful, rich, with a fancy car and a big house, but all alone and unfulfilled, trying to hold on to my own thing.

It wasn't easy getting here, but the more I see my husband needing me spiritually, the more focused I am on my purpose in life and in the marriage. I want him to know that I have what he needs to accomplish the vision God gave him. I want him to know that I am willing to sacrifice my life and my will to fit into his plans. He is the one responsible to God for accomplishing the vision. Therefore, I must be diligent on my watch and make sure I am doing my part. I may not see the rewards today, but he will complete his assignment.

It's very important that your fiancé or husband has a vision; therefore, before you get married, ask your fiancé what is his vision for the marriage. If he does not have one, he is doing you and your family an injustice. If he can't provide you with one, start praying to the Lord for Him to reveal it to your fiancé, or husband if you are already married. Your destiny is correlated to the vision. Don't get married until you know and understand what the vision is for the marriage. As a future wife, you need to know if you are willing and can submit to it.

"Where there is no vision, the people perish:" Proverbs 29:18 (KJV)

Chapter Seven

When You Find Your Purpose in the Marriage

"Call unto me, and I will answer thee, and shew thee great and mighty things, which thou knowest not." Jeremiah 33:3 (KJV)

Jeremiah 29: 11-13 states, *"[11] For I know the thoughts that I think toward you, saith the Lord, thoughts of peace, and not of evil, to give you an expected end. [12] Then shall ye call upon me, and ye shall go and pray unto me, and I will hearken unto you. [13] And ye shall seek me, and find me, when ye shall search for me with all your heart."* (In the New Living Translation Bible it says plans).

This scripture is one of my favorite scriptures in the Bible. It says that God Almighty knows the plans or thoughts He has for me. He knows my purpose and when I seek Him with all my heart, He will reveal it to me.

How do these scriptures relate to marriage? Well, since you asked, I will tell you. As I stated in chapter six, we all have a purpose. If we didn't have one, there would be no reason for our existence. Every living creature on this earth has a purpose or reason for living. Whether or not you find your purpose is up to you.

Many of us believe that our purpose is one dimensional. For a good part of our lives, we strive to obtain what we believe our calling is, only to find out that once we reach our goal, it doesn't fulfill us. And if we're honest with ourselves, deep down in our hearts, it's not what we want to do. We do it because it's easy, accessible, the money is good, it brings prestige, power, recognition, and the people who we deem important say we should.

Regardless if it's a lawyer, doctor, or CEO, if it is not what you were called to do, that thing you're trying to obtain will never complete, fulfill or satisfy you. It can't. If it's not what God created you to be, no matter how hard you want it to, all your efforts will be futile. The expensive car, the beautiful home, the prestigious career, and the designer clothes are all a mirage; a facade in an attempt to bring you the happiness you desire without God. I know. I've been there. I thought that if I achieved what society deemed pertinent, I would be complete. I did feel good for a moment achieving my goals, but they never completed me. They left me empty inside, craving for something I couldn't comprehend. I know now what I was craving for was my purpose in the Lord. I didn't realize it until I'd wasted precious years of my life.

As a Christian, it's not about you, it's all about Jesus. It's not about you or your plans; it's all about the plans Jesus has for you. I know there are songs written about doing your own thing such as, "*I Did It My Way*," yet I wonder what doing your own thing has gotten you? My question to you is, "Did doing your own thing fulfill you?"

When you become someone's wife, you can no longer do your own thing or do things your way. I reiterate, if you want to do it your way, stay single. I believe that we are here on this earth to make a difference in another person's life, and out of that, our lives become meaningful and fulfilling. Unfortunately, the world's philosophy of taking care of number one has resulted in the Body of Christ missing numerous opportunities to make a difference and rise to the occasion when called upon by God. Sadly, as women of God, our selfish ways and thinking have made it tough for Christian women to be the wives their husbands need.

Now I know many husbands make it hard, and sometimes unbearable for us to be godly wives. Yes, they too need a lesson on how to love as Christ loves the church. But, we don't focus on what they are not doing. We focus on ourselves and allow God to fix us, while we pray for them.

There is a saying, "Behind every successful man is a woman." The truth is, beside every successful man is a woman or as it pertains to this book, his wife. Eve wasn't behind Adam. She came from within him. She came from his ribs. The ribs are on the side, not the back.

"[21] So the Lord God caused a deep sleep to fall upon the man, and he slept; then He took one of his ribs, and closed up the flesh at that place. [22] And the Lord God fashioned into a woman the rib which He had taken from the man, and brought her to the man. [23] And the man said, This is now bone of my bones, And flesh of my flesh; She shall be called Woman, Because she was taken out of Man."
Genesis 2:21-23 (NASB)

When we become wives, we must inquire of the Lord about our purpose in the marriage. We must ask Him, "Lord what is it that you would have me to do? What does my husband need of me? Why did you select this man to be my husband?" And finally, "How do I fit into my husband's plans and the vision you gave him?" If we ask these vital questions in the beginning of the marital process, we won't waste precious time and years.

We want to know our future husband's bank account information, and his credit standing. We also want to know if he has a good-paying job that can support the lifestyle we want. All of these questions are pertinent; however, we also need to ask the Lord about his weaknesses, his insecurities, his past that he tries to hide, his issues, and his fears. We need to ask how our gifts and our treasures accommodate his lack. Status is important; nevertheless, his spirituality is even more important. Even if your husband doesn't know these things about himself, you need to know them to a degree, because you are his help meet. You are his wife. You have to assist him in becoming all he is called to be. This is not about his ego versus yours; it's about the success and the survival of your marriage.

I was busy focusing on me, my needs, my desires, and my goals that I almost aborted my assignment and missed the opportunity of assisting my husband in completing his assignment. It sounds drastic doesn't it? But, it's the truth. I would have never known until it was too late, or when I stood before the Lord. Being a wife is serious business in the Lord's eyes. It's more important than what I wanted to do. Notice that I said, "What I wanted to do," not what the Lord called me to do. There is a major difference. My will almost cost me my marriage. And it could've cost me my life, because whether I died physically or spiritually, I would have still been diagnosed as dead.

Pete had to get somewhere, but he couldn't get there by himself. He needed my help. I had what he needed to help him get to his appointed destination. My purpose is intertwined with his success. If he is not successful, or if he is not doing what God called him to do, how can I be successful in my pursuits? We would be working on two different planes, producing a devastating outcome, resulting in either a failed marriage, or two people living together just tolerating each other. I didn't want this type of marriage. I saw Pete's weaknesses, yet I was strong in the areas he was weak. I was to cover him with my strength as he covers my weaknesses with his strength. We are a team, husband and wife, with one focus, and on one accord.

As a wife, you are not to overpower your husband with your strengths. (Nine times out of ten, your strengths are his weaknesses. You should compensate for and cover them.) In the beginning, he may not ask for your help; he may not know he needs your help. If he doesn't ask for your help, you still need to help him. Give him your strengths. Don't manipulate, dominate, or try to control him with them. Give them to him freely, as Jesus gives them to you freely. Your strengths are designed to help another. This is why the Lord put you and your husband together. You have what your husband needs.

Now I see Pete from God's perspective. He is my husband whom I love, and he is also someone the Lord put in my life so I could help him reach his potential and destiny. Rarely do I focus on what he is not doing. I look at him and say to myself, "As his wife I have what he needs to be successful." Like Eve with Adam, I came out of him. I am bone of his bones and flesh of his flesh. When it was time for me to be manifested, God brought me out for him for us to fulfill the vision He gave Pete. My purpose and fulfillment in life are intertwined as his wife.

When I look at many successful ministries, I see something very obvious. If the Pastor has a wife, she knows her purpose. She understands the vision, and is willing to give up her plans for a season in order for him to fulfill his assignment from God. We want men such as these men. We presume they have a special potion, or they are brilliant, but these men are no different from your fiancé or husband. The difference is the wives of these men were willing to sacrifice their plans for a season. They came from within their husbands – their ribs – and answered the call of a wife. Now they are living grand, and you are pouting because you want the promises without the process.

Chapter Eight

Your Purpose Will Lead You to Serve Your Husband

"[27] And whoever wants to be first must become your slave (servant). [28] For even I, the Son of Man, came here not to be served but to serve others, and to give my life as a ransom for many."
Matthew 20:27-28 (NLT)

"But among you, those who are the greatest should take the lowest rank, and the leader should be like a servant." Luke 22:26 (NLT)

As a wife, you need to learn how to serve your husband, not be his doormat, but serve him. There is a difference. Now, I know the word serve is considered repulsive, disgraceful, and even insulting to women. It's not even in our vocabulary. In fact, it's downright demeaning to us. Why should we serve our husbands, or any men for that matter? We have great careers, fancy cars, and plenty of money in the bank. So why should we stoop down, with our dignified selves, in our designer clothes and get dirty to serve a man? After all, we are women, hear us roar. Yes, we are women and we are roaring; but, we are single, lonely and crying out to God about how we want a husband, and how badly we need a man.

The paradox in this is that we serve everyone else, our boss (who sometimes treats us as insignificant beings), our friends, our children, and our Pastors, but it's hard for us to serve our husbands. We don't see it as demeaning or inconsiderate when our boss asks us to work on a project, which requires long hours, working late into the midnight hour, and some weekends. We can't or don't say no to him. He is our boss. He gives out the promotions. It's not considered unusual if our girlfriend calls in the late hours needing to talk. We listen, laugh and cry with her. We are there for her. We serve her and don't think twice about it. She's a friend.

It's not considered unusual to serve our kids, even though, they have joined far too many after school clubs, projects, or sports teams. Since they are our children, we don't mind. We do it no matter how hectic it is to travel all over town, making sure they arrive on time, wearing us thin to the bones, demanding our time to help them with a school project they can't finish because of all the other non-school- related activities. Yet, we don't mind saying yes to their requests or serving them.

Or, how is it that when the pastor asks us to do something, we rush to serve the man of God without hesitation. (You should serve the man of God, but there is a balance even in serving him.) We don't have a problem cooking for him, baking him all sorts of pies and other goodies that he didn't request. Yes, we serve everyone, at anytime, but we can't serve our husbands. The husband we begged and pleaded to God for day after day.

When the Lord was dealing with me about being a help meet, one of the first things He put in my spirit was to serve my husband. Me, being me, I told him I did. The Lord, being the Lord, knew I was being rebellious in my comment, and told me to serve him as I served my boss. Once again, me, being me said, "But my boss pays me well. Anyway, I do serve him, what more do you want me to do?" Needless to say, the Lord made me see things His way.

When I was working for my former boss, it wasn't a problem for me to work late hours to complete projects. Whatever was needed or required of me from my boss, I did it in an exemplary manner, giving my all – 100%. It was nothing for me to work on weekends or holidays. I didn't think twice about it. Whatever my boss needed I was there to assist. I gave my all, even when he didn't call for it. I served my boss.

I thought serving Pete meant cooking, cleaning, keeping a neat and organized house, and providing him with the intimacy he needed. I did all these things, so I didn't have an earthly idea what the Lord meant by serving my husband. I didn't understand at the time I was looking at the process of serving my husband from my perspective, because in my rational thinking, I did serve him. What more did I need to do; furthermore, what more did the Lord require me to do?

As married women, how can we serve our children, parents, friends, bosses, our pastors, and others in authority before we first serve our husbands? The Lord is not pleased if you are serving others with a spirit of excellence, but you are not serving your husband in this manner. How can He be pleased with this? He is a God of order. If you are taking care of others' needs before taking care of your husband's, you are out of order.

Serving your husband is not a form of slavery. It's not bondage. In many cultures and careers, it's a high honor and privilege to be considered a servant. You wouldn't have a problem with being a servant to a prestigious dignitary, such as the President of the United States. You would actually brag to your friends about how you get to serve a man of great importance and prestige. Well, this is how the Lord wants you to serve your husband, for he too is a man of great importance, worth and prestige. He is your husband, the one the Lord gave to you. I don't care if he doesn't serve you, you serve him. Your boss doesn't serve you, and you don't have a problem with serving him. In fact, serving your boss is second nature to you.

When the Lord first told me to start serving Pete, I have to be honest, it was very hard. It appeared that the more I served him, the worse he became. In the beginning, I saw how he was messy, inconsiderate, at times sloppy, and even ungrateful. When he didn't pick up after himself after I had cleaned the house from top to bottom, it took everything I had within me to keep from slapping him on his head. Yet, I continued to serve him, while gritting my teeth and holding back my words. (I failed a lot in the beginning.) I wasn't perfect, but the more I sought the Lord for strength, the easier it became to serve my husband. I gained a new appreciation for being a servant in the Lord's eyes. (Was it worth it? I'll let you know.)

Serving your husband is honorable in the sight of the Lord. Don't allow others to ridicule you or make you feel ashamed. I guarantee you that the husbands of those women laughing wish their wives would serve them. A few years ago, I was reading a story in a magazine about a woman who sought the Lord about her unruly and mean husband. The answer she received was to serve him. No matter how mean he became, she was to serve him. From that day forward, she was always polite, considerate and nice to him. After a while, her husband took notice and began to change. Because she made up in her mind to serve her husband, today, her husband is a changed man. He is now a God-fearing man. In retrospect, what if she had paid attention to the naysayers, or the women who thought she was crazy? If she had listened to the taunting of others, they probably wouldn't be married today; or, worse he may have not gotten delivered from his vices.

Serving your husband puts you on the path to intimate relations with him. Intimacy brings renewed relationship and friendship, which results in you growing closer to each other; helping you fulfill your assignment for the marriage. The more I served my husband, the less it became a task, or a burden. I began to see my husband from a new perspective. I saw in him what the Lord wanted me to see. As a result, my love for him grew. I wasn't in bondage nor was I his slave. My love for him caused me to serve him. It caused me to help him to become what God needed him to be.

If I wanted my husband to serve me, regardless if he did or didn't, I had to serve him. For this reason, Jesus came down from Heaven to Earth to serve us, reconciling us back to the Father. Jesus, the greatest servant alive, loves us so much that He served us to the fullest by dying in order for us to live. He sacrificed His life to save us from our sins and destruction. The greatest became the least. What a servant. *"But among you, those who are the greatest should take the lowest rank, and the leader should be like a servant,"* Luke 22:26 (NLT). Jesus didn't care what people thought of Him. He did not care if they ridiculed His ways, or actions. He was about His Father's business. He came to serve. Being a servant is great in the eyes of the Lord.

How can you serve your husband? The answer is simple. Seek the One with the answers, Jesus. Through the Holy Spirit,

He will tell you how to serve your husband. No two people are alike. How you serve your husband will be different from how I serve mine. Let me forewarn you, when you start serving him, don't anticipate anything in return. Serve him simply because you love him. Remember the woman with the unruly and mean husband. It took years for her husband to change. She considered not herself, but her husband. She continued to serve him, in spite of his actions. She did not put a time limit on the Lord. She had to sacrifice her ways in order for her husband to be delivered, healed, and reconciled back to the Father. She was looking unto Jesus and not her husband. In Hebrews 12:2-3 (KJV) it says, *"Looking unto Jesus the author and finisher of our faith; who for the joy that was set before him endured the cross, despising the shame, and is set down at the right hand of the throne of God. For consider him that endured contradiction of sinners against himself, lest ye be wearied and faint in your minds."*

Jesus did not look at the current situation or circumstances. He focused on what was ahead, the prize. He endured the rejection, the humiliation, and the shame. As an outcome of His sacrifice, He is now sitting down at the right hand of the throne of God, making intercession for us. Jesus endured the cross because of His love for us. Like Jesus, you have to be willing not to look at the now. Your focus must be on the future- the things to come.

Again, your husband may not appreciate your efforts in the beginning. Worse, he may portray the macho man, taking advantage of your kindness. Regardless of what happens during the process, know that God sees everything, including your husband's behavior. If you focus on Jesus, who is the Author and Finisher of your faith, and faint not, your sacrifice won't be in vain. I am a living witness. Keep your eyes on the prize (Jesus), and the manifestation of change in your husband will come in God's timing.

Now back to the question. Was it worth it? If you asked me this question while I was going through the process, I would have said to run. It hurts, and it's not worth it. Today, I will still tell you to run if you are not ready to go through the process. However, as for me, it was worth it. The outcome is much more than I could've ever imagined.

Serving my husband and waiting for him to change was not the major outcome. The significant and dramatic change was not in Pete. It was in me. I changed. I started out as an "I" person, now it is all about "us." I don't have to be the forerunner, or the one with all the answers, the one who has to be in control. I don't have to prove anything to myself or to anyone else. It doesn't matter if I come up with the idea, and Pete gets the glory or the fame. It doesn't matter if I am overlooked because God gets the glory. Serving Pete made me see things from a new perspective. Now I enjoy being his wife, serving him, being with him, and helping him. There are no more conflicts, struggles, or battles fought. I didn't lose my identity or my personality, nor do I feel foolish, enslaved or in bondage. I feel liberated.

You see, in the beginning, it was about serving Pete. But during the process, I realized it was God's plan to make me a better person, and to bring out His best in me. As the saying goes, *"I once was blind, but now I can see."* Now I see that serving my husband and others is for my benefit. It keeps me focused, humbled and always looking unto Jesus, the Author and Finisher of my faith.

What started out as a process ended in me growing into my destiny. I gained the freedom to be the woman God created me to be. I gained the knowledge and understanding that serving my husband is beneficial to my joy and peace in the Lord. What others view as weak has made me stronger, not in my own strength, but in the strength of the Lord. The outcome speaks for itself – my husband is happy, and I can finally rest.

Chapter Nine

Sarah Called Abraham lord (With a Small "l")

"Therefore Sarah laughed within herself, saying, After I am waxed old shall I have pleasure, my lord being old also?"
Genesis 18:12 (KJV)

"Even as Sarah obeyed Abraham, calling him lord: whose daughters ye are, as long as ye do well, and are not afraid with any amazement." 1 Peter 3:6 (KJV)

My initial thought was to title this chapter, *"Your Husband is Your lord, With a Small 'l'"* but after careful consideration, I decided not to... for the mere fact that you would abruptly put the book down, burn or trash it, perceiving that I'd completely lost my mind or worse my husband had me brainwashed into a cult. Before you condemn me, first hear my appeal. Remember, I told you God's ways or thoughts are not like ours:

> *" [8] For my thoughts are not your thoughts, neither are your ways my ways, saith the Lord. [9] For as the heavens are higher than the earth, so are my ways higher than your ways, and my thoughts than your thoughts."* Isaiah 55:8-9
> (KJV)

I am not referring to the word master as if you own something, or someone, nor am I implying that your husband is your God when you call him lord (with a small "l"). What I am saying is that your husband, or the position of the husband, should be regarded with reverence and honor. If no one else respects or honors your husband, you should. Even if he is not acting honorably, it doesn't negate the fact that his position still requires respect and honor. When I was in the United States Army, I always informed my fellow soldiers that you don't have to respect the person, but you must respect the rank, or the position.

In Genesis 18:12, God told Abraham (Sarah's husband) that at this time next year she would conceive a child, a son. Sarah was ninety and Abraham was almost one hundred years of age. Upon hearing this, Sarah laughed and said to herself, (I am paraphrasing) *"My master (or lord) and I are too old to conceive a child."* (In the King James Versions she says, lord, in the New Living scripture it says master and husband. Both words have the same meaning.) The word lord in this text refers to "Adown, or Adoni- master, but not the Almighty God. This is why it's a lower case "l."

Strong's Concordance Dictionary refers to it as, 'adown, Hebrew 113, Strong's 'adown, *aw-done'*; or (shortened) *'adon, aw-done'*; from an unused root (meaning to *rule*); *sovereign*, i.e. *controller* (human or divine):- lord, master, owner. Compare also names beginning with "Adoni-."[1]

Anytime you see the word lord with a small "l" in the Bible, it is referring to lord or master; in today's language, we say boss, or leader. When we say Jesus is Lord, we use the capital letter "L," signifying that He is Lord.

---

1   Ramsey, Glen, Strong's Concordance, Reference. Apple App Store. Version 2.0.1, November 2, 2013.

To illustrate this better, have you ever seen an old movie portraying England in the seventeenth century when they spoke such words as "My lord?" They were honoring the position with respect by addressing the man as his titled signified. This is what Sarah did when she addressed her husband, Abraham. By calling him lord, she was honoring his position as her husband, or should I say her "head." Therefore, we can conclude that the word Adoni is more than a name, it speaks of relationship, and submission.

The husband is the head of the house, and he should be treated as such. This is the ordinance of God. It doesn't matter if he doesn't step up to the plate, or perform as the leader should; regardless, that is his position. I briefly spoke about order in the previous chapters. In this chapter I will go more in depth about the topic, so you'll know I haven't lost my mind. It's still intact.

Again, I want to reiterate that God is a God of order. If your husband is out of order, God will deal with him. That is not your job. Believe me, I learned the hard way when dealing in this area. Before I tell you about some of my experiences, look what Ephesians 5: 25-33 has to say about this:

> "[25] Husbands, love your wives, even as Christ also loved
> the church, and gave himself for it; [26] That he might
> sanctify and cleanse it with the washing of water by the
> word, [27] That he might present it to himself a glorious
> church, not having spot, or wrinkle, or anything; but that
> it should be holy and without blemish. [28] So ought men
> to love their wives as their own bodies. He that loveth his
> wife loveth himself. [29] For no man ever yet hated his own
> flesh; but nourisheth and cherisheth it, even as the Lord the
> church: [30] For we are members of his body, of his flesh, and
> of his bones. [31] For this cause shall a man leave his father
> and mother, and shall be joined unto his wife, and they two

shall be one flesh. [32] This is a great mystery: but I speak concerning Christ and the church. [33] Nevertheless let everyone of you in particular so love his wife even as himself; and the wife see that she reverence her husband."

Verses 25 to 32 exemplify how a husband ought to love his wife. (Again, if the husband is not operating according to the Word, he has to answer to God). It is important that the husband loves his wife; nevertheless, this is not our focus. I want to focus on verse 33, where it states that the wife is to reverence her husband. The husband is called to love his wife as Christ loved the Church. (Jesus Christ gave His all for the Church... *He died for us.*) Notice that it doesn't say a woman needs to love her husband. It says to *reverence* him. Reverencing your husband is a priority in the Lord's eyes. Love is there, or will come, depending on the reasons you got married. In essence, I believe a man does need his wife to love him; however, I believe it is equally important that his wife respects him as the head of the household.

Respecting your husband is as vital as serving him. Respect requires you to recognize he is the head of the family. He is the leader, and because of his position, he has the final word over pertinent family decisions. Respect also requires honoring him, praising him, listening to him, helping him and submitting to him. It requires unifying with him for the common good of the marriage.

Submitting to your husband is part of the marriage covenant. It does not mean you are weak, foolish, or enslaved. By submitting to your husband, it actually signifies that you are submitting to the order of God; you are reverencing and honoring the Lord and His Commandment. It takes a strong woman of faith to submit because it takes great faith and trust when you are allowing others to lead and guide you. When you are in the position of submitting to your husband, you are in order. God not only hears your prayers, He will answer them too. Of course, if your husband is out of order, or requests you do something contrary to the law, or God's commandment, you are not obligated and shouldn't succumb to his requests. Always know God is a God of order. He will never require you to do anything outside of His order or the parameters of the law.

In the beginning, for reasons I previously discussed, I had a real problem submitting to Pete. I told you it was all about me. Cooking, cleaning, and providing him with intimacy was my idea of submission, or respecting my husband. Yet, when the Lord was purging me on how to be a wife to my husband, my perception of submission was shattered to pieces. I go into great details about the process in my book, *"Helpmeet or Hindrance, Which One Are You?"*

There was one particular incident when the Lord was telling me to allow my husband to take the lead. He told me to shut up because when He told me to keep quiet, I didn't. He had to get direct with me. Anyway, Pete and a couple of people from our former church decided to venture into a multi-marketing business. We had participated in a business of this caliber in Texas; therefore, I understood how they operated. The business we had participated in Texas brought us a small success. When he first approached me with this new venture, I listened carefully. After he explained how it worked, I agreed that it would be something to invest in. However, as he got more involved, I knew in my spirit something wasn't right. When I approached him about this, he said that he believed in the business, and that I needed to support and trust him. I did. But, the more he got involved, the more anxious I felt. Something wasn't right. I couldn't put my finger on it. My spirit continued to show me I was right. As much as I wanted to gripe, complain, and tell him, the Lord had me to keep quiet. Pete made the decision, and I had to abide by his decision. The initial cost was a couple of thousand dollars, which we didn't have, but I pondered on what the Lord was telling me and restrained from saying anything. Talk about being difficult...on a scale of 1 to 10, it was a 10(+).

When we invested in stock for the business, I knew things were getting out of control. I prayed to the Lord, "Lord, I believe in my heart and spirit that something isn't right, but since Pete wants to continue in this, I'm asking that whatever amount of money we put into the business, we will get it back. We won't lose anything but time." Well, it turned out that something wasn't right. One by one, people started realizing that it wasn't going to make them rich. Having invested a lot of money into the business, some of them opted out, while others were forced to quit, losing a great deal of money. When Pete realized it wasn't going to work he stopped too. We didn't lose anything but time. All of the money we put into the business, we got back. We came out even. Unfortunately, others didn't. I believe that since I respected and honored the order of God, and allowed my husband to make the final decision, God honored and answered my prayer.

I wish I could tell you it got easier from there, but it didn't. Pete still made some bad choices, causing us more setbacks. A few times I would tell him, "I told you so" or "You are wrong," and not in a sweet way. The more I addressed him in this manner, the more he tuned me out, even though he knew I had a good track record. I had to learn to shut up and let him take the reins (or the steering wheel) and enjoy the ride, even when the ride got bumpy. I had to learn to respect his position as the head. I had to realize in this marriage, ordained by God, he was my lord, with a small "l." I couldn't go against the order of God. I had to learn to go to the Lord and pray instead of murmuring and complaining about the decisions he made, whether they were right or wrong in my eyes. I also prayed for my husband. As always, the Lord honored and answered many of my prayers, or gave me the peace to maintain through the storm.

It's easy for wives to take over, or tell their husbands they are wrong. But it takes courage to allow them to make the final decisions even when knowing it's not the best decision in the end. The courage is not in our faith and trust in our husbands. It's in our faith and trust in the Lord. There will be times you can't help him (which we will discuss in the next chapter). The best thing you can do for him is to pray for him, while respecting his position as the "Head" of the marriage. As you do this, the Lord will honor your tears and frustration, and He will give you peace while He works on your husband. You cannot be your husband's Savior. Jesus is his Savior. So, always know that when your husband does enter into error, when he comes to himself, the Lord will deliver him out of it, and restore him.

I leave you with this to ponder: On two different occasions, Abraham, out of fear of his own life gave his wife to other men. One is in Genesis 12:12-20 (KJV. The other can be found in Genesis 20:1-18 (KJV):

> *"[12] Therefore it shall come to pass, when the Egyptians shall see thee, that they shall say, This is his wife: and they will kill me, but they will save thee alive. [13] Say, I pray thee, thou art my sister: that it may be well with me for thy sake; and my soul shall live because of thee. [14] And*

> it came to pass, that, when Abram was come into Egypt,
> the Egyptians beheld the woman that she was fair. [15]
> The princes also of Pharaoh saw her, and commended her
> before Pharaoh: and the woman was taken into Pharaoh's
> house. [16] And he entreated Abram well for her sake: and
> he had sheep, and oxen, and he asses, and menservants, and
> maidservants, and she asses, and camels. [17] And the Lord
> plagued Pharaoh and his house with great plagues because
> of Sarai Abram's wife. [18] And Pharaoh called Abram, and
> said, What is this that thou hast done unto me? why didst
> thou not tell me that she was thy wife? [19] Why saidst
> thou, She is my sister? so I might have taken her to me to
> wife: now therefore behold thy wife, take her, and go thy way.
> [20] And Pharaoh commanded his men concerning him: and
> they sent him away, and his wife, and all that he had."

In each incident, Sarah knew her husband was in error; however, instead of complaining or telling him off, as many of us would've done, she respected his position and decision as her master. She submitted. Sarah's trust and faith were not in her husband. Her trust and faith were in her God. She knew her husband was crazy to have even considered this insane plan, yet she couldn't go outside of the order of God; therefore, she went with the other men. I believe on both occasions, as Abraham schemed up these foolish plans, she immediately went into warfare prayer. She interceded for herself and her husband, and the Lord delivered her out of the arms of another man both times. Because of her willingness to submit and respect the authority of her husband, her treasure chest became more bountiful. Abraham was always given more in the end than what he had in the beginning.

Yes, I know this is a far-fetched example, especially with Sarah agreeing to her husband's plan, but you get the picture. The bottom line is that when you reverence your husband, God is pleased. He will answer your prayers accordingly, and always give you the peace to maintain you throughout the storm.

Chapter Ten

Your Husband Needs a Wife

"[24] On the journey, when Moses and his family had stopped for the night, the Lord confronted Moses and was about to kill him. [25] But Zipporah, his wife, took a flint knife and circumcised her son. She threw the foreskin at Moses' feet and said, "What a blood-smeared bridegroom you are to me!" [26] (When she called Moses a "blood-smeared bridegroom," she was referring to the circumcision.) After that, the Lord left him alone." Exodus 4:24-26 (NLT)

A man needs a wife. He doesn't need a girl, a caretaker, or a mother. He doesn't need a woman who cannot be a wife. Again, there is a difference. Yes, a woman is a female; however, she may not have wifely qualities or attributes. She may have the sex appeal, the charisma, the flair, the personality, and the drive to be successful, but if she can't put aside her womanly traits, not femininity, and be a wife to her husband, what good is she to him?

Many times, as wives, we do not understand our role or responsibility. I believe we can't and don't because we have not been properly taught, not in a biblical perspective anyhow. We have been instructed on how to be homemakers and supporting wives to our husbands. We are trained how to clean, cook, nurture, make and keep the house perfect, to look beautiful, to smile, and be intimately prepared for him. We are trained and taught everything, except how to be his wife. I believe that's why many of us are messed up, alone and frustrated, pretending to be something we're not, while on the inside we are screaming for help.

Yes, I do believe cooking, cleaning, etc. are significant to the marriage. We don't need to stop doing those things. Although they are vital and necessary, I like to think they are, as a job description would say, other duties assigned. Unfortunately, we have caused many women to become distraught, or burned out because they can't be the perfect wife as society dictates. We do everything by the book as it pertains to being a wife, and yet, we are still at the same place we were when we first got married. We are attempting to be Mrs. Perfect. We are imitating art, instead of being what God designed us to be. Trying to imitate art is becoming a "*Stepford Wife.*"

I have news for you, there is no perfect wife. What you see in the magazines or on television are all illusions. They are figments of our imaginations vying for our attention in order to obtain something that is unobtainable. And you know why there is no perfect wife? Because there is no perfect husband. We are all individuals in God's eyes. We have similarities, but we are different, with different assignments. One woman's gift is cooking, whereas another woman's gift is administration. It's unrealistic and unfair for a person who is called to be a great chef to attempt to make others be what she is called to be. They can't. We all can't cook as well as Julia Child. No matter how hard we try, our beef wellington will not taste as good as hers, especially if cooking isn't our thing. That's her gift, not yours. We need to stay in our lane, and drive our own cars.

My husband doesn't need me to be what magazines or famous people say I should be. He needs me to be *his wife*, and sometimes I failed him. Yes, he was responsible too, but as his wife, I had to do my part. When I knew that some of the decisions he was making were not wise, as his wife, I should have intervened and prayed for him through the leading of the Holy Spirit. When he sometimes needed to fall, I never allowed him to because I didn't want him to get hurt. Inadvertently, I became the man because I wouldn't let him be the husband. When things got hard and he wanted to quit, instead of encouraging him, and pushing him to finish, I told him that it was okay not to finish because I would always be with him. (In reality, I wasn't, though I didn't know it until I had my complaining moments).

Remember when I spoke about your husband needing your strength, well, I didn't give Pete my strengths. My strengths were what he needed, not necessarily my cooking or cleaning skills. If I gave him what he needed, all the rest would follow. Are we happy? Yes! Is it perfect? No. People often perceive us as newlyweds, even though we have been married for over twenty years. Whether we're happy is not the issue. We both have specific roles in the marriage. Pete has an assignment that is from the Lord. The Lord sent me as his wife to help him the assignment.

The Lord knows Pete's weaknesses. He knows his schisms, isms, and all of his other issues.

The Lord, knowing Pete's weaknesses and my strengths, chose me to be the wife for Pete. My strengths are designed to help Pete fulfill his assignment. The Lord chose me to be Pete's help meet, not hindrance. If I am to help him, I must obey the Lord. Even if it means sometimes letting him fall. If I don't do this, I'll hurt him in the long run instead of helping him. The mother of the boy can't make him into the man God called him to be, or help him complete his assignment. The Lord gave that authority to the wife, and no one else. This is why the scripture states in Genesis 2: 23-25 (KJV), "*[23] And the Lord God said, It is not good that the man should be alone; I will make him an help meet for him. And Adam said, This is now bone of my bones, and flesh of my flesh: she shall be called Woman, because she was taken out of Man. [24] Therefore shall a man leave his father and his mother, and shall cleave unto his wife: and they shall be one flesh. [25] And they were both naked, the man and his wife, and were not ashamed.*" (As his help meet, if I allowed Pete to get off course without doing my part, I was accountable too.)

I don't care if your husband is mean, moody, or even stubborn. As his wife, you have more power than you think. You have the Lord on your side. Who do you think the Lord is going to answer first? The mean, stubborn husband or the God-fearing, praying wife who is being a help meet to her husband? You, of course! Don't forget, the Lord knows your husband's weaknesses. That's why you are married to him. If you know he is wrong, deal with the discomfort, let him sulk and pout, and let him fall if he has to. The Lord will pick him up when he comes to himself, and he will. As long as you continue to nurture or baby him, he will never be the man he is called to be. He will continue to be a momma's boy, or worse a weak man. And in this case, you are acting like his momma, and not his wife.

By the way, what's a momma's boy? Simply put, it is a grown man who still acts like a boy. On the outside, he looks like a man, but internally, he still is a boy. We call men such as these "momma's boys" because their mothers won't loose them from their apron strings. They still want to breast feed them. These women think they know what's best for their sons, even though their sons are grown men. They don't. I say to these women, let the boy become a man and stop hurting and hindering him by enabling this type of behavior. When he is ready to get married, his future wife is thinking she's getting a man, but all she's getting is a momma's boy.

Mothers fail wives when they don't allow their sons to become men. When they do everything for them, even after they are grown, they are hurting everyone involved. They fail to understand that their sons are not little boys anymore, and that their constant and continuous interference in their lives keeps them from being the men God and their wives need them to be. (By the way, a woman can't teach a man how to be a man. It's not in her DNA).

A Word of Wisdom: To all the mothers who still allow their sons to hold on to their apron strings, when your son gets married, his first priority is his wife, not you. To all the future wives, you better make sure that when you walk down the aisle, there's a man waiting for you, and not a momma's boy.

This goes for a wife too. When you get married, he is your husband, not your son. He doesn't need a pacifier. He needs to be a man. Again, you are not his protector, his redeemer, or his Savior. He doesn't need you to treat him like a child by telling him what to do, where to go, or what to wear. Yes, there are times when you will tell him what to do or what to wear, but as his wife. Your husband doesn't need your approval. He needs you to be his wife, not his mother. Don't get the roles mixed up.

I always tell people that I am not Pete's mother, I am his wife. His mother can't do the things I do to him or for him.

Listen to what I am saying with your spiritual ears. In order for your husband to get to his destiny, sometimes he has to fail. When you do everything for him, there is no challenge. It's easy to for him to become idle, or complacent. He has to fall. He has to cry out in desperation to the Lord when he can't figure things out. Again, as his wife, you are not your husband's Savior. Jesus is his Savior. Jesus has the answers to his questions and dilemmas. Your solution is temporary, and it may backfire. Jesus' answers are permanent. They always lead to destiny and fulfillment.

Please understand that as a wife, you don't have to say you're strong to be strong. One of your greatest strengths is knowing that you are. You don't have to prove anything. It's sad how many women in the twenty-first century are deceived into thinking that women are stronger, better and smarter than men, that they need us, but we don't need them. That's a deception from the enemy. We are deceived when we believe that we need to handle the home, the business, the budget and the children. We are deceived into believing that without us, men are lost. We are deceived when we think that we have it going on more than they do, that we are more together, focused, successful, educated, and spiritual. We are Eve; we think we know what's best. No, we don't voice this out loud, but in our hearts, as we continue to go up the corporate ladder, receiving larger paychecks, and buying anything we want to buy, this is what we are conveying. They are the weaker vessel, not us. And now, the roles have been reversed. They start assisting us in our goals and dreams. They are on the sidelines, cheering us on, while we are running with the ball, scoring the touchdowns. Again, we are not to become doormats, or slaves or in bondage. This is not the reason why God created us. We must comprehend the connotation of being a wife. We are their help meets; they are not ours.

I know this is a hard pill to swallow. I know there are men who believe the wife doesn't have a voice in the marriage, and she has to submit to everything he says. He is the "King of His Castle." I have news for men who feel this – you are wrong, and if you don't get it together and repent, you are going to have to answer to the Lord. Again, that is why I stress that when a man comes asking for your hand in marriage, you better know it's the Lord. Otherwise, this man will cause you some real harm and set-backs.

Submission is a beautiful thing when you are following God's way. I know we have been taught from the pulpit, but I dare to say, the majority of the teaching is from a religious perspective and not a spiritual one. In submission, there is never bondage, control, manipulation or intimidation. As a matter of fact, both the husband and the wife are to submit unto one another. We don't often hear this version of scripture from the pulpit: *"Submitting yourselves one to another in the fear of God,"* Ephesians 5:21 (KJV). Regardless, even if we don't hear this from the pulpit, we do know that as the wife submits to her husband, her husband is responsible for loving her as Christ loved the Church:

> *"[25] Husbands, love your wives, even as Christ also loved the church, and gave himself for it; [26] That he might sanctify and cleanse it with the washing of water by the word, [27] That he might present it to himself a glorious church, not having spot, or wrinkle, or anything; but that it*

should be holy and without blemish. [28] So ought men to love their wives as their own bodies. He that loveth his wife loveth himself."
Ephesians 5:25-28 (KJV)

Nowhere in the scriptures will you find Jesus abusing, mistreating, or threatening the church. He was and still is about Love. I close with the scripture I started the chapter with, Exodus 4:24-26 (NLT):

"[24] On the journey, when Moses and his family had stopped for the night, the Lord confronted Moses and was about to kill him. [25] But Zipporah, his wife, took a flint knife and circumcised her son. She threw the foreskin at Moses' feet and said, "What a blood-smeared bridegroom you are to me!" [26] (When she called Moses a "blood-smeared bridegroom," she was referring to the circumcision.) After that, the Lord left him alone."

The Lord gave Moses the assignment of going to Egypt to tell Pharaoh to let God's people go. Along the journey, Moses became ill. It states in the scripture that the Lord confronted Moses and was about to kill him. Moses' wife, Zipporah, knew why this was happening. According to God's covenant with Abraham, Moses was supposed to circumcise his son. For whatever reason, Moses did not. Moses couldn't go to Egypt and fulfill his assignment because of his disobedience. Zipporah, seeing that her husband was in disobedience of God's covenant, and in danger of aborting the assignment and losing his life, performed the circumcision rituals on her son. After completing the deed, she threw the blood-stained foreskin at the feet of her husband. When she did this, the Lord left Moses alone and Moses carried out his assignment.

For a woman of Zipporah's status and background, this was a repugnant act. However, even though Zipporah did not want to do this, as a help meet to her husband and to save his life, she performed the repulsive ritual. If she hadn't, we wouldn't be reading about Moses in the Bible today.

At that moment, between life and death, Moses didn't need anyone to enable him, appease him, weep for him, or put the pacifier in his mouth. He didn't need someone who was going to sit back and let him die, while complaining and murmuring about why he didn't circumcise his son. He didn't need someone who was going to point the finger at him, telling him I told you so, or calling him names out of his character. Moses needed a wife. He needed a wife who would get down and dirty with him, forsaking her position, her status, her clothes, and her dignity, if needed. He needed a wife to help him with his assignment. Zipporah was the wife he needed.

Final Thought: Sometimes if a wife is not doing her part, it can cost her husband his purpose, his destiny, and even his life.

Chapter Eleven

Looking From the Outside of the Man
(What You See Is Not Always What You Get)

"For my thoughts are not your thoughts, neither are your ways my ways, saith the Lord. [9] For as the heavens are higher than the earth, so are my ways higher than your ways, and my thoughts than your thoughts."
Isaiah 55:8-9 (KJV)

As women, when praying to the Lord about a husband, we tend to focus on the external characteristics or qualities we want in a man. We tell God our prerequisites for a husband. We want him to be tall, dark and handsome, with black hair, brown hair, blond hair, blue eyes, or brown eyes. We want him to have a good-paying job, to be generous with money, gentle, loving, kind, affectionate, understanding and compassionate. We want him to be perfect, our knight in shining armor, or our prince charming, who beckons to our every need, wish and command. We want him to come to the table with a full-course dinner; even though, we know we can't provide the dessert. How hypocritical of us to want him to have it together when we don't. Truth be told, many of us are not half of what we want him to be. We want the prince, while we're still the ugly stepsister.

There is a saying that goes, "What you see is what you get." There is also another saying, "First impressions normally tell you about a person." I am glad God does not live by these foolish sayings. If He had, Rahab, the prostitute wouldn't be in the lineage of Jesus Christ (Joshua 2:1 and Matthews 1: 1-17). Neither would Tamar, for she too played the role of a harlot and was also named in the lineage of Jesus Christ (Genesis 38 and Matthew 1:1-7). The Lord looked past their now, and saw what they would become.

We are quick to judge others by our first impressions of them. First impressions are inaccurate gauges of a person's total being. We are deceived when we believe that a person's economic status makes him either successful or less fortunate. How we dress, talk, what we drive, what school we attend, or the type of house we live in, signifies the person we are thought to be. I know this not by observation, but by personal testimony. There are occasions when I go into a store impeccably dressed, yet broke to the core, and I am waited on with dignity and respect. On other occasions, when I have plenty of money to spend but didn't feel like dressing up, I am treated as if I am undesirable and insignificant. When this happens, I approach the management with my concern, who apologizes profusely to me. However, it doesn't matter because the damage was done. They judged me inaccurately and unjustly.

There are people who live above their means, perpetrating a royal lifestyle, while living from paycheck to paycheck. They are on the border of financial ruin. However, they are treated with respect and dignity because of their appearance, or should I say masquerade. Whereas, you have an individual who doesn't dress stylishly, drives an older car, and appears less fortunate, is treated and judged as if he is insignificant; yet, this person has more money in the bank than the majority of people. We're broke trying to keep up with the Jones' while this individual is leaving a legacy for his children and his children's children. A prime example is Sam Walton, who built the Wal-Mart Empire. Based on first impressions, he was an average Joe. How inaccurate. Today, his children are all billionaires, and their children will be too. What a legacy.

As for being judged, I remember purchasing my first designer bag. I am not materialistic, nor am I into name brands, but I do love quality clothes. I shop wherever I see quality and a bargain. At the tender age of forty-five, I purchased a designer bag. I never would have purchased an expensive item such as this, but my oldest sister April, who I admire, purchased this particular bag. She is the most level-headed of all of my siblings, me included. She's very sensible with her money, so if she purchased one, I knew it was cool and worth the investment. I noticed since purchasing this bag, I'm treated with more respect. I've actually observed this in action. People who wouldn't normally speak to me began to speak to me and hold conversations. They looked at the bag and perceived that I had it going on. What they failed to see is I don't have it going on, not in their perspective anyway. In God, I do have it going on, but the reality is I'm just another person with a designer bag. What they see is not what they really see.

If we look at the outside of a person, what they have, what they're driving, what school they attend, or what type of job they have that's all we are going to see. That's called superficial. What matters is not the exterior of a person, but the interior of a person. Yes, he has it going on in the looks and finance departments, but on the inside, he's a manipulator, womanizer, an abuser, and he's afraid to commit. However, we don't focus on these internal things. All we care about is that he has money, and he's good-looking. That's what's important. Yes, in the beginning these things are important to you, but at some point in the relationship, when you are miserable, hurt, rejected and abandoned, and crying out to the Lord to take the pain away, they aren't important anymore.

I love the Lord. Do you want to know why? I'll tell you why. He sees my good, even when I am bad. He sees my future and not my present. He knows my potential, even when I don't know it, or others don't see it. He doesn't judge me. He picks me up and gets me back on track. We all have been judged, including me. And I've also judged others unjustly. It hurts when you are judged by others, especially significant others, and although we don't like being judged, we judge all the time. When we look at another person differently because of their ethnicity, race, or economic status, we are judging them.

By the way, as Christians, we are not to judge. Jesus says in Matthew 7:1-2, "*[1] Judge not, that ye be not judged. [2] For with what judgment ye judge, ye shall be judged: and with what measure ye mete, it shall be measured to you again,*" and also in Luke 6:37, "*Judge not, and ye shall not be judged: condemn not, and ye shall not be condemned: forgive, and ye shall be forgiven.*"

Jesus came to earth not to condemn or to judge, but to save it. His purpose was to reconcile us back to the Father. He knew we were not perfect. We were born of sin; therefore, He didn't focus on what we were, but what we would become.

"For God sent not his Son into the world to condemn the world; but that the world through him might be saved." John 3:17 (KJV)

I know of one incident where I was at a very vulnerable state in my life. Someone based my whole make-up as a person on where I was at that moment in my life. This person did not know me, but assumed that she did because of where I was. A person does not have the ability or foresight to know you after the first five minutes of meeting you. That person may be accurate in some areas, but getting to know the real you will take time. There are occasions, for ministry sake, and for warning, when the Holy Spirit provides vital information to you about the person, but this doesn't make you qualified to say you know all about that person. I am not getting too deep. I am making you think. I have been with myself for almost fifty years. Every day, with the help of the Lord, I am still learning new things about myself, some good, some bad, and some ugly. It's a process.

Many of us tend to focus on past and present events to shape our view on life. How we view these two categories can determine the outcome of our lives. It is our natural instinct, our make up to want to see a thing before we can believe in something. We need to know what we are getting into before we begin. Basically, we walk by sight and not by faith. In doing this, we tend to choose the easy way, because we feel comfortable and know what to expect in the end. We single out people we have things in common with or who we are comfortable being around. We don't want to go outside of our comfort zones. As women, we want the husband with the successful career, the nice car, and plenty of money in the bank; and, if he has looks, we hit the jack pot.

The Lord, on the other hand, sees and knows all things. He sees the beginning and the end. Before the beginning of a thing, there is an end. In other words, the end was finished before the beginning began. Therefore, when you decide to walk with the Lord, through trust and faith, many times in the beginning and during certain seasons in your life, you don't know where you're going, or where He is leading you. It's a faith walk. That's why Hebrews 11: 6 states, *"But without faith it is impossible to please him: for he that cometh to God must believe that he is, and that he is a rewarder of them that diligently seek him."*

When you are praying for a husband, you have to have faith in God and believe He knows the right person for you. He sees the beginning, the end and the middle. While we see and focus on the beginning, God sees the trials, tribulations, pain, heartaches, and disappointments. He sees the changes in our physical posture, the many roads we will travel, and the many obstacles we will face and overcome. So, if you are not connected to the right person, these things can lead you down paths of destruction, sin and maybe an early death.

As I previously stated, when the Lord was preparing me to become someone's wife, a few men came into my life. They were all handsome with successful careers, and some were wealthy. On the outside, they had everything I desired and that society said I should look for in a husband. Yet, having traveled that road before, I knew that they were not the ones for me. You see, even though these men pursued me, promising all of the material "stuff" I longed for as a woman, I had to seek the Lord and inquire about them…*"Lord, is he the man for me?"*

Many times we get so caught up in the pursuit that we don't inquire of the Lord about the one pursuing us, causing us to marry out of the will and timing of God. The Lord knew these men weren't for me; I had to know. I couldn't base my judgment on what they could give me in the natural. I had to base everything on what the Lord wanted for me.

Proverbs 3:5-8, The King James Version states that we should: *"Trust in the Lord with all thine heart; and lean not unto thine own understanding. [6] In all thy ways acknowledge him, and he shall direct thy paths. Be not wise in thine own eyes: fear the Lord, and depart from evil. [8] It shall be health to thy navel, and marrow to thy bones."*

I know that we think we know better, and that we have the wisdom for the answers we need. There are times we do, but the majority of the time, we don't. For something as significant as marriage, many times, we don't. I'm in no way guaranteeing that by seeking the Lord before saying, "I do" that your marriage will not end in divorce. I can't. People change, and things change. Sometimes people stop putting their faith in God. What I am saying is that when your marriage is established and ordained by the Lord and is Christ-centered, chances of having a successful marriage are better. When the Lord has yoked you together, it's harder to tear you apart or divide you.

> *"And said, for this cause shall a man leave father and mother, and shall cleave to his wife: and they twain shall be one flesh? [6] Wherefore they are no more twain, but one flesh. What therefore God hath joined together, let not man put asunder."* Matthew 19:5-6 (KJV)

I know in a previous chapter I told you how Pete and I met. Now I'll tell you the entire story. When the Lord was preparing me for my husband, Pete, He kept me hidden, and though others tried to find me, they couldn't. Towards the end of my preparation phase, the Lord started telling me my husband was coming. It was similar to the story in Matthew 25 about the ten virgins, when someone cried out, "The Bridegroom is coming." When the Lord started telling me, I had no idea what was going on. I knew it couldn't be my ex-husband because he had recently gotten married again, and I was no longer in love with him, or wanted the marriage to be resurrected. That was my past, and it was over.

The day I met Pete was just another day, or so I assumed. My friend invited me to go to a Gospel concert one evening. I tried to get out of it, but she was very persuasive. She had purchased the tickets a while back, so she couldn't get a refund. I finally gave in, not because of her persuasion, (and she was good) but because somewhere in the back of my mind something told me I needed to go. Looking back, I know it was the Holy Spirit guiding me to my destiny.

I didn't see Pete from the front, because we were sitting a couple of rows behind him. What I did see were his hands. His hands were praising God in a manner that connected to my Spirit. I didn't know how he looked, or what he did for a living, but I knew something was different about him because of his hands and how they praised God. He was with a fellow soldier from my Battalion. (Today he and his wife are our mentors and special friends.) After the concert, I stopped my friend to say hello, and I believe that's when he introduced me to Pete. I don't recall anything after that. My friend, who I went to the concert with, jokingly says when Pete and I first met, everyone and everything else ceased to exist. We literally had eyes only for each other. Today, after all these years, we still do. To say we fell in love at first sight sounds as if I'm fabricating the truth, but that's exactly what happened. We fell in love and have been since the first time we met.

I didn't want to fall for Pete, not in the beginning anyway. (Although, that only lasted a couple of days, because within days, I was totally head over hills!) Yes, he was tall and handsome, and I liked him very much, but he wasn't the type of man I wanted to marry. I wanted someone older, more established, and with money. I wasn't a gold digger, nor did I want someone to take care of me. I was a successful officer in the army. I owned my home. I had purchased a new car, and I had a little money in the bank. I was on my way to being established and comfortable, and I wanted someone to help me reach my goals. Pete, on the other hand, was a Staff Sergeant, Non-Commissioned Officer (NCO). He drove a used BMW—an older version. He lived in the barracks, and he didn't have a lot of money. What he portrayed on the exterior told me to run. I didn't. Something about him was different than any other man I had encountered before. I didn't see the exterior of a man. I saw what the Lord showed me in the Spirit – *the potential of a man*. Not what he was, but what he would become.

A few people tried to talk me out of marrying Pete. He was after all a Non-Commissioned Officer, and I was an officer destined to do great things in the Army for Uncle Sam. It was also considered fraternization. However, I knew something inside of me said he was my husband. To make sure I was hearing from God, I sought wise and mature godly counsel from every aspect of my life, my family, my elders and deacons at church, my peers, and even my commanding officer, who was a devout Christian.

To say it has been a bed of roses would be telling a fib. During the twenty years (+) of marriage, we have had many trials, disappointments, obstacles and hurdles to overcome. He lost his mother and three aunts. I lost my grandmother, my grandfather and a few other relatives. We had to overcome financial setbacks that would've caused even the best marriages to crumble. I am still going through fertility issues, while still believing God for the child we both desire. We both made many wrong choices that caused us some setbacks. I had to learn how to submit and be his wife and help meet. He had to learn how to be my husband. Through it all, and I mean all–bankruptcy, setbacks, you name it– our love continues to grow stronger. What should have pulled us apart only intensified the bond and love we share for each other and more importantly the love and trust we have in God. Each issue or problem we have encountered has made us better for each other and better servants for God and His Kingdom.

If the Lord hadn't put us together as husband and wife, we wouldn't have made it through the storms. Being the type of woman I was, and being the type of man he was, we would have called it quits. I would probably still be in the military doing my own thing. But, the Lord knew we could weather the storm because we are a threefold cord (The Lord, Pete and myself) that is not easily broken (Ecclesiastes 4:12). We didn't focus on what we saw in the natural, we focused on where we were going- what we didn't see.

Many of us want the benefits of being a wife now instead of working through the process to obtain them. What will it profit you if you get the prize money now if you don't know how to spend it? Nine times out of ten, you'll be wasteful and frivolous. You will not appreciate the contents behind the prize. What would I have profited if I did it my way? What would it have cost me in the end? It would've cost me my blessings, my wonderful husband, and my destiny in God. It would've cost me my joy, my peace and my fulfillment. God knew the end of a thing before the beginning began. *"For what shall it profit a man, if he shall gain the whole world, and lose his own soul?"* Mark 8:36 (KJV).

We say we want the Lord to bring us a husband. We say we will wait on Him, and whomever He chooses for us we'll marry. What if He chooses someone with a criminal past who is now converted into His Kingdom. What if He selects for you a person who has a blue-collar job, and you have a white collar career with a six-figure salary? What if He selects a person who has a different background than you, or someone who is the complete opposite of you? Suppose the person is not as handsome as you want him to be? Suppose the person is a different ethnicity, but still a Christian? Would you still say yes? Always know that the Lord is not going to send you anybody. He is going to send His best for you. He knows the gifts you have collectively and individually. They will accomplish the plans He has for you and the marriage.

How many times have we said "no" and missed our blessings because they didn't fit into our plans? We were looking at them from a worldly perspective, rather than a spiritual one. Our husbands could be right in front of our faces, waiting on us; but, we can't see him because we are still waiting for Prince Charming, who, by the way, is never going to come.

We want to see it visually, but we fail to comprehend that what we see is rarely what we get.

This scripture says it all: *"But people who long to be rich fall into temptation and are trapped by many foolish and harmful desires that plunge them into ruin and destruction,"* 1 Timothy 6:9 (NLT)

Chapter Twelve

Seeing the Man From Within

"But the Lord said unto Samuel, Look not on his countenance, or on the height of his stature; because I have refused him: for the Lord seeth not as man seeth; for man looketh on the outward appearance, but the Lord looketh on the heart." 1 Samuel 16:7 (KJV)

The outside of a man seldom reveals the true man. It takes a special woman, his wife, to get to know the real man within her husband. However, many women don't want to take the time to discover that person. They tend to focus on the exterior of the man and base their relationship or his character on what they see in the natural, not realizing that the interior of the man is the real man.

Women will say, "If only my husband or fiancé was a certain way. If he only acted this way, I'd be happy." As women, we have so many ifs. "If only he was more sensitive. If only he cuddled or listen more. If only he wasn't so rough around the edges." Or how about this one, "If only he would change." What we are doing is looking at the outside of the man, instead of the inside of him.

Women have often told me how wonderful and nice my husband is to me. How much they admire our relationship. I look at them and say thank you. These women are seeing the aftermath. They see the results of me getting on my knees, with tears in my eyes, praying to the Lord about my husband. Praying for Him to open his eyes, to move him into his destiny, or to get him where he needs to go in the Lord. What I want to say to them is you don't know the whole story. If the truth be told, it was, and still is, a work in progress. Many of us are not willing to commit to the process. All men have rough spots around the ears, the face, or whatever. They are men. As the wife, you need to learn how to tap into the roughness and bring out his gentleness.

I was no different than many wives when it came to complaining about my husband. I wanted him to change to fit my standards, and my feelings of what he should be for me. I used to want what I saw in other marriages. I wanted Pete to enjoy shopping with me. I wanted him to pray more with me. I wanted him to be more, or in my case, overly, sensitive to my needs. The Lord had to show me that I wasn't married to these other men. I was married to Pete, and he was sufficient for my needs. I had to learn, no matter how much I wanted Pete to enjoy shopping with me, shopping isn't his cup of tea. Sure he goes with me on some occasions and doesn't give me the mall face as often, but he doesn't enjoy shopping, not even for himself; whereas, I do. When I came to that conclusion, and accepted him for who he is, and stopped trying to change him, he started going shopping with me. However, he can only stomach it for a few hours.

Pete may not enjoy doing some things that I thought he needed to do for me. Notice I said, "What I thought he needed to do for me." But, when it comes to a scratch anywhere on my body, he notices it right away. Many times before I do. He notices the little things that mean much more to him and our marriage. I had to get this, and you do too. It is easy to look at another marriage and think they have it together, while yours is going down the drain. Before you jump to conclusions or wish your marriage was like another woman's, you need to ask her to show you her scars and bruises, because all marriages have scars and bruises. Some are healed, whereas, some are scabbed over. Regardless, they all have a story to tell.

If you focus on the exterior of your husband, and never see the real man, the internal man, you have missed a vital aspect in your marriage. As the wife, it is very significant that you get to know the internal man as equally if not more than the external man. The old me would not have accepted Pete for a husband. Yes, he was tall and handsome, but in the natural he didn't bring anything to the table, or so I perceived. How fortunate of me that I didn't base my decision on becoming his wife on my fallible standards. I would have lost out big time. Thank goodness I saw inside of the man. Yes, his outward appearance was rough around the edges, but it was my job as his future wife, with the assistance of the Holy Spirit, to bring out his inner man. I was not to reflect on what I saw from the outside as a result of his background, values, upbringing, intellectual, or economic status. I couldn't judge him based on those factors. Nor could I base my perception of him on my standards, my family's standards or the standards of society. I had no right to do this. I had to focus on what God showed me about my husband: his potential, what he is destined to be. My assignment as his wife is to help him reach his full potential. That's why you need to pray for your husband.

As wives, it's easier to point the finger and blame our husbands when things go wrong. A husband doesn't need a wife to do this, to call him out of his character, or emasculate him. He needs his wife to be there for him and with him, through the good and through the bad. Believe me, he knows his choices were wrong. He knows he made a mistake. What He doesn't need is for you to remind him of his mistake for the rest of his life. He won't tell you what he needs verbally, but I'll bet you he is telling you with his actions. You just haven't been watching.

I've told you that my husband has not always made the right decisions, and sometimes his choices or decisions cost us. Yes, sometimes I did complain, and would say to him, "I told you so." Was I correct or justified in my actions? No, especially in the way I communicated my thoughts to him. Regardless of how good it felt at the time, I was still in error. I am not proud of how I handled every situation, but not once did I put my husband down or call him out of his character. He was my husband, and more importantly a man of God. I still had to respect the order.

There are women who put their husbands down after they have made a few mistakes, not realizing they are human, and are imperfect vessels such as themselves. It's funny, they will call their husbands fools, but I wonder what would happen if their husbands called them fools? By the way, if you call your husband a fool, what does that make you since you married him? Your husband is not a fool. Nabal was a fool. "*This man's name was Nabal, and his wife, Abigail, was a sensible and beautiful woman. But Nabal, a descendant of Caleb, was mean and dishonest in all his dealings,*" 1 Samuel 25:3 (NLT).

Never call your husband outside of the name God calls him. Nabal was a fool. He was a mean and dishonest man. Hopefully, this is not your husband, or husband-to-be. (If this does describe your husband, or fiancé, I encourage you to pray without ceasing. God is still in the miracle business). Your husband may not be focused, or he may currently be going in the wrong direction, but he is still a man of God. He is not a fool. Your husband is a Saul, waiting to be converted into a Paul. Remember how Saul was in the beginning? Believing he was doing this in honor of the Lord, Saul killed Christians. How wrong was he! Thank goodness God didn't focus on the exterior of a man, or on what everyone else saw. The Lord saw the interior of a man, a Paul within a Saul, waiting to be birthed. Well, that is how it is with your husband. If you focus on what you see now, Saul, you will never see the Paul in him. It is your job as his help meet not to think you are better, more spiritual, or even more educated. It is your job, with the assistance of the Holy Spirit, to bring out his interior.

Remember when the Prophet Samuel had to go and anoint another king in place of Saul? Samuel went to the house of Jesse and saw Jesse's eldest son, Elias. Because of his outward appearance, Samuel thought he was the next King of Israel. But, the Lord didn't choose Elias, or any of the other sons present. The Lord chose the one with the ruddy good looks who took care of the sheep to be the next King of Israel.

> *"[6] And it came to pass, when they were come, that he looked on Eliab, and said, Surely the Lord's anointed is before him. [7] But the Lord said unto Samuel, Look not on his countenance, or on the height of his stature; because I have refused him: for the Lord seeth not as man seeth; for man looketh on the outward appearance, but the Lord looketh*

on the heart. [8] Then Jesse called Abinadab, and made him pass before Samuel. And he said, Neither hath the Lord chosen this. [9] Then Jesse made Shammah to pass by. And he said, Neither hath the Lord chosen this. [10] Again, Jesse made seven of his sons to pass before Samuel. And Samuel said unto Jesse, The Lord hath not chosen these. [11] And Samuel said unto Jesse, Are here all thy children? And he said, There remaineth yet the youngest, and, behold, he keepeth the sheep. And Samuel said unto Jesse, Send and fetch him: for we will not sit down till he come hither. [12] And he sent, and brought him in. Now he was ruddy, and withal of a beautiful countenance, and goodly to look to. And the Lord said, Arise, anoint him: for this is he. [13] Then Samuel took the horn of oil, and anointed him in the midst of his brethren: and the Spirit of the Lord came upon David from that day forward. So Samuel rose and went to Ramah."

1 Samuel 16:6-13 (KJV)

The Lord sees the interior, or countenance of a man's heart. He sees what the man will become with the proper training, guidance and direction, and not what he is now. It took Moses over eighty years to be the leader he needed to be to lead the children of Israel out of captivity: forty years in the palace and forty years in the wilderness. It took David many years before he became the King of all of Israel. Paul had to be deprogrammed from the Saul mentality before he became Paul, the man who wrote the majority of the New Testament. Each of these men had to go through the necessary character-building steps before being used mightily by God. So does your husband. He has to be taught, trained, pruned and put through many tests. Even Jesus had to wait thirty years to start His ministry– His purpose for coming to the earth. He had to be prepared, trained and groomed to carry the cross and the sins of this world.

I couldn't understand back then why the Lord started telling me to pray for Pete and to be his wife. I understand now. Today, he is a man after God's own heart. I see a man of integrity, vision and purpose. A man growing into what God has called him to be. I see a man being used mightily by God. I see my husband; the husband God has called him to be for me. I see the internal man.

Look at your husband or fiancée and tell me what you see. Now, look at yourself, and tell me how this reflects you. Are you an asset or a liability?

Chapter Thirteen

Preparing For One Night With Your King

"And the king loved Esther above all the women, and she obtained grace and favour in his sight more than all the virgins; so that he set the royal crown upon her head, and made her queen instead of Vashti." Esther 2:17 (KJV)

When preparing to be a wife, I recommend that you read the Book of Esther. It's about one woman's journey and the process she had to go through to become a wife to the King of Persia, who by the way, was the ruler of the world at that time.

After reading Esther again, I detected something I've never seen before. Many commentaries, movies and books have depicted Queen Vashti as insubordinate to the King. When you read the book contents and don't understand what the Spirit is showing you, it appears that she is. But was she? Or was she doing what was expected of her by following the protocol and customs of that era?

The Book of Esther begins with King Xerxes giving a feast (or banquet) to celebrate his reign as the ruler of his kingdom. (He had a celebration that lasted for almost six months. This was the feast to end the celebration). Everyone was invited, from the greatest to the least, the noblemen, officials and the people of the kingdom. In the middle of the feast, having had too much to drink, he called for his wife Vashti, the queen, to come. He wanted the people to see and admire her great beauty.

Now, while the King was having his celebration, Queen Vashti was having her own celebration for the women. (This right here should enlighten you that she was following protocol, for while her husband was having his feast, she was having a separate feast for the women. Therefore, it's within sound reason to conclude that she was not invited to attend his feast. How can I say this? Easy. If she was, she would've been in attendance. What wife do you know would not be there with her husband, helping him celebrate a victory in his life?) When she was summoned by the king's messenger to present herself before the king and his guests, she knew what the king was asking of her was against protocol. She would've been disgraced if she had gone. Adhering to protocol, she refused the king's request, or summons. Her refusal resulted in her being banned from the kingdom.

Was she correct to disobey the king's summons? Should she have gone, even though it was against protocol and let the King deal with the dilemma he caused? After all, he was the king, and he had the authority to go against protocol. That's one to ponder on. Whether right or wrong, she lost her position.

In situations such as Queen Vashti's, sometimes as a wife there will be occasions to keep the peace, you have to submit to your husband's leading, even though you know he is not leading you or the family in the right direction. You have to learn what battles to fight in order to win the war. How do you win? By maintaining the marriage. War is costly, and all battles are not worth the casualties. Again, I am not talking about if your husband asks you to do anything that is against the law, or against the order of God and His commandments, or if he is being abusive. I am referring to a man of God, requesting or doing something that you know isn't right in your spirit, but won't result in devastation, destruction, or demise. On occasions such as these, you have to keep quiet, pray and let God fix the problem. God will either change your heart, or change your husband's heart. Remember, *"The heart of the king is in the hands of God. The Lord guides it wherever He pleases,"* Proverbs 21:1. Sometimes we have to learn obedience through our suffering. Queen Vashti didn't understand this. Yes, she was the queen, but she wasn't the king.

How does this relate to you and the Book of Esther? In Romans 8:28 (KJV) it reads, *"And we know that all things work together for good to them that love God, to them who are the called according to his purpose."* This was the case with Esther. God used the situation with Vashti to get Esther into the palace for the appointed time. He knew what was going to happen in the future.

Now before a new queen was selected, every maiden scheduled to see the king had to go through one year of purification. *"Now when every maid's turn was come to go in to king Ahasuerus, after that she had been twelve months, according to the manner of the women, (for so were the days of their purifications accomplished, to wit, six months with oil of myrrh, and six months with sweet odours, and with other things for the purifying of the women,"* Esther 2:12 (KJV). Each young maiden had the same opportunity and chance to be the next queen of Persia; however, only one would be chosen. How they chose to prepare for the king would determine who was selected. That is the same with many of us. Again, we tend to focus on the wedding day, or being a bride instead of focusing or learning how to be a wife to the man we are about to marry.

It took over a year for Esther to spend her one night with the king. During her time of waiting, she was in preparation. She was being hidden. During the waiting process, the Lord was preparing her to reign as a queen; but, more importantly He was preparing her to be a wife to the king. As a result, everywhere she went Esther found favor. She was admired by everyone who saw her. Hegai, the King's eunuch was very much impressed with her; he showed his favoritism by indulging her in special privileges such as a special menu and extra beauty treatments. He also assigned her seven maids chosen from the king's palace and moved her and the maids into the best place in the harem (Esther 2: 9). When it was Esther's turn to go before the king, she accepted the wisdom of Hegai. Hegai told her what gift to take to the king. Esther was taken to the King at the royal palace in early winter of the seventh year of his reign. The King loved her more than any other young woman, thus declaring her queen in place of Vashti (Esther 2:15-18).

Esther was chosen out of thousands of beautiful women to be the next queen. Have you ever wondered why? Yes, she was beautiful, but I wonder how many others surpassed her in beauty? Why was she selected out of thousands? What did she have that the others didn't? In regard to your husband, this is what you should be wondering too. Why did your husband select you from all the others? What did he see in you that made him request your hand in marriage? Why did he want you for his wife?

What was special about Esther, other than her beauty? It's quite simple. She was available and submitted to God. She allowed God to select her husband for her. In her waiting and preparation period, Esther learned how to have the heart of her husband first, before she had the heart of the king. If Esther didn't have the heart of her husband, she couldn't have gone against protocol to ask him to save her people, the Jews. Esther was beautiful, but she was also a very wise woman. She wasn't preparing for the wedding day. She was preparing for the days after. Her preparation was fulfilled and manifested when she had her one night with the king. He loved her more than any of the others because he didn't see a bride; he saw someone ready to reign with him. He saw his wife.

Esther learned everything about her soon-to-be husband during her waiting period. What she didn't know, she took the wisdom from one of the king's most trusted servants, Hegai. She didn't have any idle time, playing or gossiping with the girls. She wasn't busy planning the wedding. She was learning how to be a wife. She knew that role was more vital than one day; for the wedding is not the main attraction. The minister doesn't say to the man, "Do you take this woman as your bride?" He says, "Will you take this woman as your wife?"

If you focus on being a bride, you'll never get past the day. When the honeymoon is over, and the days turn into years, you're wondering what happened along the way. You ask yourself, "What happened to the man I married? What happened to the man who, when I walked down the aisle to the tune "Here comes the Bride," thought I was the epitome of beauty? The man who promised me the earth and everything in it. Where did he go?" Well, he's right there with you. When you were walking down the aisle, you should have been looking at your husband, not a groom.

I told you that before I married Pete, the Lord was preparing me to be his wife. If I had focused on being his bride, we wouldn't have made it. In my preparation stage, I was learning about the long haul of marriage and what it took to be a wife to my husband. When the storms came, the bride in me wanted to run away, but the wife in me had to fight to keep me and my marriage together. The wife in me was trained for the long haul. I realized that satan wanted to destroy my marriage. See, the storms and trials were never about me; they were about our marriage and our destiny. As with Esther, in my waiting period, I was being prepared for the good and the bad.

Your marriage is bigger than the both of you. That's why the Bible says a man that finds a wife, finds a good thing. The good thing is from the Lord. The Lord has prepared the wife to weather the storm. Was it hard when we were going through? Yes! However, the more we went through, the closer we became to each other and to God. God saw the big picture. I had to go through the preparation. Likewise, with Esther. She also had to go through the process. The Lord had to prepare Esther to be a wife to a king. He needed someone who would submit to His will, and intercede for His people. He knew that there would be a person during that time period, an enemy of the Jews, plotting to wipe them out:

> *"[3] Then the king's servants, which were in the king's gate, said unto Mordecai, Why transgresses thou the king's commandment? [4] Now it came to pass, when they spake daily unto him, and he hearkened not unto them, that they told Haman, to see whether Mordecai's matters would stand: for he had told them that he was a Jew. [5] And when Haman*

saw that Mordecai bowed not, nor did him reverence, then was Haman full of wrath. [6] And he thought scorn to lay hands on Mordecai alone; for they had shewed him the people of Mordecai: wherefore Haman sought to destroy all the Jews that were throughout the whole kingdom of Ahasuerus, even the people of Mordecai. [7] In the first month, that is, the month Nisan, in the twelfth year of king Ahasuerus, they cast Pur, that is, the lot, before Haman from day to day, and from month to month, to the twelfth month, that is, the month Adar. [8] And Haman said unto king Ahasuerus, There is a certain people scattered abroad and dispersed among the people in all the provinces of thy kingdom; and their laws are diverse from all people; neither keep they the king's laws: therefore it is not for the king's profit to suffer them."

Esther 3:3-8 (KJV)

When Mordecai and the rest of the Jewish population heard this, they wept bitterly before the Lord (Esther 4:1-4). He went to Esther for assistance. At first, Esther refused his request because it went against protocol, but Mordecai's powerful words changed her mind:

"[13] Then Mordecai commanded to answer Esther, Think not with thyself that thou shalt escape in the king's house, more than all the Jews. [14] For if thou altogether holdest thy peace at this time, then shall there enlargement and deliverance arise to the Jews from another place; but thou and thy father's house shall be destroyed: and who knoweth whether thou art come to the kingdom for a time as this?,"

Esther 4:13-14 (KJV)

Esther was chosen for that appointed time because she understood the heart of her husband. It was never about one night with the king. It was about her destiny with the king. The difference between Vashti and Esther was that Esther understood this and Vashti didn't.

Chapter Fourteen

What Are You Bringing to the Marriage?

"A wise woman builds her house; a foolish woman tears hers down with her own hands."
Proverbs 14:1 (NLT)

None of us are perfect. We all have flaws and imperfections. That's why we need a Savior. In marriage, because you are dealing with two imperfect vessels, before you say, "I do," allow God to deal with you, to deliver you, and fine-tune your imperfections. Don't bring anything, "junk" or "mess" that will hinder the marriage from being profitable and a blessing. Don't bring baggage to the marriage, bring luggage. There is a difference. Baggage is something you bring from where you have been; luggage is what you use when you are planning to go somewhere.

Webster's dictionary defines baggage as: (1) the traveler bags and personal belongings of a traveler, (2) Things that get in the way. [2] Luggage seems similar to a degree, but it's not. It is defined as containers (suitcases) for carrying personal

---

2 "Baggage." Def. 1. Pg. 38. *Merriam-Webster's New Dictionary of the English Language.* 2001. Print

belongings.[3] Container is the sub word of contain, which means to restrain, to have within hold.[4] When you bring baggage into the marriage, you are bringing stuff that gets in the way, causing more harm than good. With luggage, your "stuff" is contained and refined. It's securely locked away in a safe container that you have taken care of.

If you don't believe that there is a difference between luggage and baggage, check out the airport one day and notice the type of luggage people carry, the regular bags versus the designer or durable luggage. Notice how the baggage handler handles both. The more expensive the item is, the more the attendant handles it with special care, especially if it's a designer parcel, such as Louis Vuitton. Now, observe how the attendant handles every day, ordinary, rundown bags. He throws them on the plane or on the conveyor. He doesn't care. That baggage isn't significant.

Here are some examples of baggage we bring to the marriage:

1. *Drama*: Whether it's baby mama, mama, girlfriend or family, drama is still drama. Remember the order of the marriage: God, husband & wife, kids, etc. When you bring in elements outside of that order, you are playing with fire.

    a. <u>Baby Mama Drama</u>: No man wants baby mama drama. If you both have extended families from previous relationships, discuss everything before you get married. Put everything on the table– the good, the bad, the possibilities and even the personalities of the previous relationships. It's better to do it before the marriage rather than after the

---

3   "Luggage." Def. 1. Pg. 309. *Merriam-Webster's New Dictionary of the English Language.* 2001. Print
4   "Contain." Def. 1. Pg. 114. *Merriam-Webster's New Dictionary of the English Language.* 2001. Print

marriage. I wasn't ready to become an instant mother to someone else's kids. You better know if you are, because once you are married, his children become your children and should be treated as such. Also, set boundaries for all outside factors, such as visitation rights, parental responsibilities, and disciplining the child or children. If you have a child from a previous relationship, understand that your husband has the right to discipline your child. Do not take your child's side against your husband, especially if your child is out of order or being disrespectful to your husband. If you do this, you're out of order. If your husband has a child from a previous relationship, be aware that the mother of the child is a vital part of his life. Often times they are going to have to talk on the phone or in person about their child. There will be times when you are not included in the conversation. You have to be secure within yourself and your marriage to handle those times. Finally, don't allow anyone from you or your husband's previous relationships to disrespect either of you. Again, discuss everything before you say, "I do."

b. <u>Mama Drama</u>: We talked about his mother letting him grow up, now let's talk about your mother. You are his wife, not your mother. Your husband is not married to your mother. Your mother, or his mother, other than motherly advice or godly wisdom as it pertains to marriage, should not have a voice in your marriage. There will be times when your mother provides advice or wisdom about marriage in general, but she should never tell you what to do based on what she did. Why? She is not married to your husband; she has her own husband.

Your husband and your father are two different people, with different personalities, upbringings, backgrounds, and assignments. Read very carefully: your mother should not have a voice in your marriage if she is negative, or has issues or strongholds herself. Finally, never allow your mother to talk about or disrespect your husband in any way. Though she is your mother, and biblically speaking you must always honor her, your husband is your priority, not your mother.

c. <u>Family Drama</u>. Today, we are experiencing more family drama than ever before. The right thing to do is to help your family in need, but not if it takes away from your family or the order of God. If it's a constant and continuous cycle of bailing your family members out, whether financially or any other need, it will cause stress on your marriage. People make choices, good and bad. It's not fair if you are always helping people recover from the bad choices they've made. I know it sounds harsh, but God is not a God who deals in emotions and guilt games. He is a God of order and not chaos. If you're always helping or bailing out family members, particularly the same ones, you need to consider why and how this is affecting your marriage. Everyday life is stressful enough; you don't need other people to bombard you with their stress and problems, especially if this is a continuous cycle, and they caused their problems. Seek the Lord on how to handle this and allow Him to show you the way, and how to say "no."

d. <u>Girlfriend Drama</u>: Keep your girlfriends, but remember your marriage has priority over them. I know there are many shows in which characters put the girlfriends before the husbands; they are wrong. If you wanted to continue hanging out with the girls, you should have stayed single. This is harsh, but true. Paul writes that when you are married, you have to care for the needs of your partner:

"[32] In everything you do, I want you to be free from the concerns of this life. An unmarried man can spend his time doing the Lord's work and thinking how to please him. [33] But a married man can't do that so well. He has to think about his earthly responsibilities and how to please his wife. His interests are divided. In the same way, a woman who is no longer married or has never been married can be more devoted to the Lord in body and in spirit, while the married woman must be concerned about her earthly responsibilities and how to please her husband."

1 Corithians 7:32 - 34 (NLT)

Don't allow your girlfriends to have a voice in your marriage, particularly if they're not married. You may not want their advice; it may cause you heartache in the end, if you know what I mean.

2. *Strongholds*: Whatever your issue is, deal with it before the wedding. I'm not telling you to be perfect, but don't go into the marriage when you know you have some real strongholds that you haven't pulled down or allowed God to deal with them. You know the strongholds I'm referring to: controlling, manipulative, bossy, and independent to the degree that you are still going to do your own thing, even though you are married. How about this stronghold;

you know everything and nobody can tell you otherwise. Need I say more? We all have some form of these issues; however, if any of these areas I pointed out have you in bondage, you are not ready to be a wife. You are not ready to relinquish the reins to a real man because you want to be the man. Wait until God delivers you, transforms you, and heals you from your strongholds. It's not fair to your husband. I reiterate, whether we want to admit this or not, the man is the head, not the other way around. God cannot go outside of the parameters of His Word.

3. *Financial Baggage*: Some areas are:

   a. <u>Shopaholic</u>: First of all, I can relate to this, because I began to shop all the time. I was spending money we didn't have. The issue wasn't that I liked shopping. The issue was why I was shopping like a "mad woman," buying things I couldn't afford; and to be honest, didn't like. Once I got to the root, I realized that I was attempting to cover up the problem I was struggling with, and shopping allowed me to suppress the real issue. If you are shopping all the time, buying things you already have, don't need, or can't afford, seek the Lord and ask Him why. Once He reveals it to you, ask Him to deliver you. Many times we shop to cover up something that's bothering us. We're putting a band-aid over an open wound without cleaning it, causing it to become infected. Furthermore, shopping a lot can keep us from our purpose. It's a set up from satan to keep us busy with "stuff" instead of doing what God called us to do. This goes for all vices.

b. <u>Debt:</u> Remember the commercial about the elderly woman falling and she couldn't get up? This is you in debt. You fell and you need God to get you back up, or to restore you financially. Prior to the marriage, inform your husband about all of your financial woes, including if you have ever filed bankruptcy, or in the process of filing bankruptcy. Don't tell him after the honeymoon, or when he opens up a bill from a collection agency addressed to the both of you about a debt you both now owe. It's not fair to him or to you if the shoe was on the other foot.   Better yet, before you get married, pay off all of your debt, and shred all of your cards except one or two. You determine which ones. (I recommend you select the one(s) with the lowest interest and least limit). Live according to this budget and be free again.

c. <u>Your Money:</u>   I emphasized ***your money*** for a reason, because it's not yours anymore. Once married, it belongs to the both of you. Don't believe me? Ask the courts during a divorce proceeding. The money between the two of you is known as "community property." There is nothing in the scripture that states the husband's money belongs to the both of you, but the wife's money belongs to the wife. However, it does say that the two shall become one, Genesis 2:24 (KJV), *"Therefore shall a man leave his father and his mother, and shall cleave unto his wife: and they shall be one flesh."*

If you are a better manager of money than your husband, you manage the money. Don't forget to set up a savings plan and other financial investments for the future. Be careful about secret accounts. Always remember God is not in the deception business. Now, if you and your husband agree to have separate accounts that's different. The bottom line still is your money is not yours. The money between the two of you is used for the good of the marriage and to manage the household. Therefore, if your husband needs money to pay the bills, and you have it but don't help out, you are wrong; especially if he is a good man who takes care of you. Get your heart right in this matter before you get married. Again, if you want to keep your money, don't get married.

4. *Emotional Baggage*: Some strongholds that deal with our emotions are:

   a. <u>Insecurity</u>: Insecurity comes from your past. It stems from people telling you that you are nothing, or you will never amount to anything. It also stems from your perception drawn from what society thinks of you. For example, you are an "Ugly Betty," meaning, you're not pretty enough, slim enough, or smart enough. The list goes on. Insecurity also derives from self-pity. However it came into existence, you need to deal with it prior to marriage. Always know that whatever you bring into the marriage, even your hidden inner emotions or issues are a part of the marriage. Allow the Lord to heal and deliver you from them prior to getting married. If you believe getting married is going to make you secure, you are dead wrong. The insecurity is hidden now, but sooner or later it's going to find its ugly way out of the closet. You must be secure within yourself before going into marriage. Your husband needs a whole and secure wife. He needs someone who is confident and happy with herself. He needs someone who has come to grips with all of her issues and body flaws. After all, no one is perfect.

b. Jealousy: As women, whether we want to admit this, there is some jealousy in all of us. Don't believe me? Let your husband start talking to a beautiful woman in your presence. Even though it's innocent, our eyes are open and our claws are drawn. Don't let this beautiful woman be dressed to kill and we are not looking our best. I believe this type of jealously is normal. We are guarding our investment. The jealousy I'm referring to is the type of woman who demands total and undying devotion from her husband twenty-four hours a day, seven days a week. She has to know where her husband is at all times and who he is with. She doesn't allow him to have any friends, and definitely not friends of the female gender. This type of woman checks his cell phone, his pockets, and his car. Need I go on? You get the picture. If you have this type of behavior, no matter how beautiful you are, I guarantee that you will always have problems. No man likes to feel like he is under a microscope and can't be trusted. If your husband is in ministry, or in a leadership position, he is going to communicate with women, and some of them will be drop-dead gorgeous. If you don't deal with your issue, you may drive him away. If you are an obsessive jealous woman, there is a reason for this obsession. There is something deeply rooted in you that you've hidden so well you don't know it's there anymore, and it's causing you to behave in this manner. Maybe you have been hurt badly by another man, and having trouble trusting again. Whatever it is, seek the counsel of the Lord and some mature godly saints. Don't bring this spirit into the marriage. It's very damaging.

c. <u>Envy/ Covetousness</u>: This is the mentality of *"Trying to keep up with the Joneses."* I have news for you. The Joneses are broke. Now that I've made you smile, let's talk about this issue. Envy is a painful awareness of another's advantage over you. It's covetousness with extreme desire for what another person has. I believe we all get caught up in envy at one time or another in lives; yet, I am not referring to those moments. I am speaking about the woman who has an extreme case. It is a daily battle for her to be the prettiest, the best dressed, and the best in everything. She always has to be seen and heard—the center of attention. This woman cannot fathom the thought of someone having a better house, car, career, family, ministry, or life than her. This stronghold must be dealt with before the wedding, because envy can cause financial ruin and marital discord. If you are struggling with this, there is something within you causing you to behave to this extreme. Ask the Lord to reveal the real issue, and to deliver you from this spirit, because if you continue to feed this spirit, you'll never be happy. Soon, you'll start looking at your husband in a different manner. You may look at him with disgust, because he cannot keep up with the Joneses. This will only make him feel like less of a provider, emasculating him from his God-ordained position. And since he wants peace in his house, he is going to do everything possible to make sure you get what you want.

d. Spoiled Little Princess: Your husband needs a queen, not a spoiled little princess, or a brat, to put it lightly. Fathers spoil their little girls. After all, they are princesses in their eyes. It's okay for the dad to give in and spoil his daughter. That's his little girl. Although you are a daddy's little girl, when you get married, you'll become someone's wife. Pouting and throwing temper tantrums were okay as a little girl, but not when you are a wife. If your husband cannot get you the pretty dress because of tight finances, he can't. Don't throw a fit, or close the bedroom door (you know what I mean) to get your way. Be careful, you are operating in the spirit of witchcraft. Don't dishonor, or disrespect your husband by always calling your father (or others) when he can't get you what you want. Give him the respect and honor to be a man. If there is a real need, allow your husband to call your father– man to man. And a real need is not a new dress, or something you can do without. Your father didn't always have it all together. He had a wife, your mother, who helped him become the man he is today. Paul says in 1 Corithians 13:11 (KJV), *"When I was a child, I spake as a child, I understood as a child, I thought as a child: but when I became a man, I put away childish things."* Put away your "little girl" attitude and be the wife your husband needs.

e. <u>Selfishness</u>: To some degree, this is in the same category as a spoiled little princess; however, you can be selfish but not spoiled, so I have separated the two. We are all selfish to an extent. It's part of our sinful nature. Even though we are saved, we have to work on not being selfish. We are selfish when it comes to our family, our time, and our money. The selfishness I am referring to is when a woman cannot think of anyone else but herself and her desires. She is selfish to such an extreme that she has to have her way all of the time. She doesn't care about what her husband wants or needs. It's all about her, and her wants and needs. This type of woman is a hindrance to her husband, because not only is she selfish, but she also has the tendency to be controlling and manipulative when she can't get her way. She only cares about what she can get out of the marriage. She'll never help her husband fulfill his assignment. It is not fair to your husband if you bring this into the marriage. Marriage is about compromise and sacrifices. It's about more giving than taking. If you and your husband are in a constant battle, vying for control, what type of marriage do you have? You have to ask yourself, why am I selfish? Why do I have to have my way? Why do I always want to be in control? Don't get married before finding out the answers and solutions to these questions.

f. <u>Fear</u>: For many of us, we are immobilized by our fears. We just hide it well. No one knows, other than God and ourselves. Fear causes a marriage to become complacent and stagnant. Some fears that can hurt a marriage are: fear of the unknown, fear of change, or monetary fears. For example, you had a poor upbringing, and even though the Lord has blessed you financially you're not able to get rid of the poor man's mentality. This type of fear is not healthy for a marriage. I know wives who don't want to change for whatever reasons (strongholds in their lives). Their husbands are caught up in the grips of their fears. They want to move forward, but they can't because their wives are not allowing them to, not with words, but with their actions. The husband will never get to his appointed destiny in Christ at this point. And, if the wife is not careful, her husband may start resenting her.

As women, sometimes we think we know what's best for our families. Our kids are in school, our house is almost paid for, or we don't want to leave our families or friends. All of these factors are important to our security as a wife, and as a woman. However, if the husband is adamant about the change, and you know he is definitely hearing from the Lord, it's time to fit into your husband's plan. Always remember, as a daughter of the *"Most High God,"* God can keep you from falling and stumbling. He guides us with His Word and by His Holy Spirit. He is never going to lead you anywhere you're not supposed to go. Yes, change is scary, but it is also healthy. It keeps our eyes on Jesus Christ, the Author and Finisher of our faith (Hebrews 12:2). It keeps us on our knees, praying, and trusting in Jesus. God wants to take your marriage somewhere– to its appointed destiny, but you're holding the timeline up with your fear.

As far as fear, I leave you with three thoughts: (1) Having fear is sin. It's saying that you trust yourself and the prince of this world rather than God. (2) You will never know where the Lord is trying to lead you, until you succumb to your fears and allow Him to lead you to your destiny. (3) If you take fear into your marriage, you are crippling your husband's destiny and your destiny too. *"For God hath not given us the spirit of fear; but of power, and of love, and of a sound mind,"* 2 Timothy 1:7 (KJV).

5. *Sexual Baggage*:

If other women have told you to use sex as a weapon to get what you want from your husband, they are giving you unwise counsel. Your husband needs sex. It's part of his make-up. He needs it for stress relief and to make him feel good. Once married, your body doesn't belong to you, and vice versa. His body belongs to you, and your body belongs to him.

> *"[3] The husband should not deprive his wife of sexual intimacy, which is her right as a married woman, nor should the wife deprive her husband. [4] The wife gives authority over her body to her husband, and the husband also gives authority over his body to his wife. [5] So do not deprive each other of sexual relations. The only exception to this rule would be the agreement of both husband and wife to refrain from sexual intimacy for a limited time, so they can give themselves more completely to prayer. Afterward they should come together again so that Satan won't be able to tempt them because of their lack of self-control."*
> 1 Corithians 7:3-5 (NLT)

If you are married and using sex as a weapon, you are operating within the spirit of witchcraft. (This isn't applicable if you are being abused physically or sexually. This is not God's will. I'm referring to women who know what they are doing.) Women who use sex as a weapon, or their kids or jobs as excuses to keep from being intimate with their husbands are wrong. If you are sometimes too tired for sex, that's understandable; but, if you're withholding sex all the time, you shouldn't have gotten married, because this is one of the purposes of being a wife. As far as being tired, try this. When your husband is in the mood and you're not, start praying for strength in the Spirit. You'll be surprised how fast the Lord gives you the strength and endurance to satisfy your husband, and in the end, you'll be satisfied too. Don't allow satan anymore control in this area.

In summary, there are many types of baggage we bring to the marriage. I've provided you with just some examples. Marriage is challenging and requires a lot of work. When you allow outside forces to come into the marriage to control, manipulate and influence it, you are giving access to the enemy. Satan's job is to steal, kill and destroy the marriage. He doesn't want you to have a fruitful and blessed marriage. He wants you to have an unproductive and unsuccessful marriage.

Whatever your stronghold is, deal with it before you get married. Don't bring baggage, your "junk" or "mess" into the marriage. That's why I plead with future wives or women who want to get married to get to know _you_. Get to know the person God created first, before entering into the Holy Covenant of Marriage. Get to know your strengths and your weaknesses. You don't want to deal with another person's issues, what makes you think your husband wants to deal with yours? Deal with your strongholds by seeking the face of God, getting into His Word, and seeking wise and mature counsel. We pull down strongholds by the Word and with the Word:

"[3] For though we walk in the flesh, we do not war after the flesh: [4] (For the weapons of our warfare are not carnal, but mighty through God to the pulling down of strong holds;) [5] Casting down imaginations, and every high thing that exalted itself against the knowledge of God, and bringing into captivity every thought to the obedience of Christ; [6] And having in a readiness to revenge all disobedience, when your obedience is fulfilled."

2 Corithians 10:3-6 (KJV)

If you do this, your foundation will be solid and well-built, giving you a higher success rate for a healthy marriage.

Chapter Fifteen

Bring God's Fruit of the Spirit to the Marriage

"[22] But the fruit of the Spirit is love, joy, peace, longsuffering, gentleness, goodness, faith, [23] Meekness, temperance: against such there is no law. [24] And they that are Christ's have crucified the flesh with the affections and lusts. [25] If we live in the Spirit, let us also walk in the Spirit." Galatians 5:22-25 (KJV)

Marriage is a divine institution designed and created by God to bring Him glory. In God's eyes, marriage is a replica of Christ and the Church, His Bride. In Ephesians 5:25-32 (KJV), the Apostle Paul writes to husbands and wives:

"[25] Husbands, love your wives, even as Christ also loved the church, and gave himself for it; [26] That he might sanctify and cleanse it with the washing of water by the word, [27] That he might present it to himself a glorious church, not having spot, or wrinkle, or any thing; but that it should be holy and without blemish. [28] So ought men to love their wives as their own bodies. He that loveth his wife loveth himself. [29] For no man ever yet hated his own flesh; but nourisheth and cherisheth it, even as the Lord the church: [30] For we are members of his body, of his flesh, and of his bones. [31] For this cause shall a man leave his father and mother, and shall be joined unto his wife, and they two shall be one flesh. [32] This is a great mystery: but I speak

concerning Christ and the church. [33] Nevertheless let everyone of you in particular so love his wife even as himself; and the wife see that she reverence her husband."

A husband is to look to Christ to see how he is supposed to treat his wife. Christ loves His Church so much He sacrificed His life for Her. Because the Church is portrayed as female, as with any groom, Christ is going to make sure He takes very good care of His precious Bride. In the scriptures above, the husband has a list of things he is required to do for his wife; however, I reiterate, the wife has only one that is pointed out. She is to reverence her husband.

If you are unable to do this, you may not be ready to be a wife. Be mindful, if you attempt to do this on your own, the likelihood of failure is almost guaranteed. The only way to accomplish this is by submitting to the authority of Jesus, and allowing the Holy Spirit within you to lead and guide you. Even if your husband is not doing what he is commanded to do, that's not an excuse for you not to submit. You must submit to the Word of God as it pertains to the husband and wife relationship.

Without the Lord, I'm not able to love my husband and submit to his leadership, especially when I feel he is off course. To be frank, there are those rare times when I don't like him, and don't want to be around him. And that's okay, because no matter what, I still love him. I have learned to reverence him in all situations, the good and the bad.

In hindsight, you can always tell a new bride. She has a lot to say. She has all the answers, and you can't tell her anything. I call her a neophyte. She's experiencing the bliss of the newly matrimonial state that we call, "The Honeymoon Years." She'll soon discover the honeymoon doesn't last forever. Her prince will turn into a man who belches, scratches, and "hogs" the remote control. One day she'll look up and notice her scars from the marriage. (Side note: The honeymoon doesn't last forever, but you can live in a honeymoon state of mind, even in the storm. It's how you perceive the storm.)

I'm not saying that a new bride doesn't have a grasp of the marriage concept. I'm saying she doesn't have enough scars to show that she's married for the long haul. Show me your scars, and I'll tell you what battles you been through. After twenty years of marriage, I have been in some battles, and I have the scars as proof. Not physical, per se, but scars on my knees from praying to God in the midnight hour to fix things. I have tear scars that you can't camouflage. I have bruises in my soul because sometimes it hurts so badly that the Lord has to come down from His throne to patch my wounds.

Again, marriage is for the long haul. It's not for the weak and feeble. It's not for people who have to be in control. It's not for the ones who can't put their egos aside, nor is it for the ones who can't sacrifice their lives for another to live. Marriage is serious and should be looked upon as such. That's why I look to the older couples who have been married for years. They have the scars. They have battle stories that I want to hear. They know how to fight when the enemy attacks the marriage. They are not full of talk. They are full of God's wisdom.

My grandparents were married for sixty-five years; over half their lives they were married. My in-laws, before my mother-in-law went home to be with the Lord, were married for over forty-seven years. They loved each other dearly, but they still had scars. My grandmother would always fix my grandfather's plate. She never worried what the other women did with their husbands, nor was she concerned with what they said about her. At the dinner table, we couldn't eat until my grandfather sat down. She had his coffee mug waiting for him, and she poured his coffee into his mug. She made sure my grandfather was taken care of. Did my grandfather acknowledge my grandmother for what she did for him? Yes! He loved her very much and made sure that she didn't want for anything within his realm. She never went without. Even in his death, he provided well for my grandmother. Did she have scars? Yes, plenty of them, but she was in it for life. One thing about my grandmother was that she didn't say much about being a wife. She didn't have to. Her actions spoke louder than her words. Today, all we do is talk. We have the Internet, Facebook, blogs, and Twitter talking about our problems and our issues. We are all talk with no solutions. And while we are talking, satan is scheming. His mission is to destroy Christian marriages. If we look at statistics, it appears he's accomplishing his job.

Jesus knew that you would have scars, and yet, He still looks at the Christian marriage as a replica of how He is with His Bride. Why? Because Jesus has the scars to prove that He's in His marriage for the long haul, too. He endured the cross so that we can live. He didn't take the easy way out. He didn't look for other options. At one time, in the midst of His praying, it had gotten intense, He sweated tears of blood. Through the tears, the pain, and the anguish, He relinquished His will, and said, "*Father, if thou be willing, remove this cup from me: nevertheless not my will, but thine, be done,*" Luke 22:42 (KJV)

Jesus saw His Bride waiting for Him at the altar. His love for her allowed Him to endure the ridicule, the persecution, the frustration, the hurt, the pain, and the rejection. Jesus knew it was worth the scars.

In marriage, we want convenience. We want the fringe benefits of being married. And yet, when the laughter ceases, and the tears and storms come (and they will), we don't want to endure. We want to call it quits. We want to go our separate ways, claiming irreconcilable differences. When adverse situations, trials and tribulations come, that's when we have to focus on Jesus and His scars. We have to look unto Jesus, The Author and Finisher of our Faith. In those times, you have to put on the whole armor of God and know that you are not wrestling against flesh and blood, but principalities in high places. You have to focus on the "Fruit of the Spirit: love, joy, peace, longsuffering, gentleness, goodness, faith, meekness, and temperance." You have to bring the Fruit of the Spirit to the marriage:

1. _Love_. We have to love in spite of the situation or circumstances. For God so loved us, He gave His only-begotten Son, Jesus, reconciling us back to Him to live in eternity with Him. He continues to love us unconditionally, even when we are disobedient, unfaithful and rebellious. He loves our good and our bad. He loves us in the worst of times, and in the best of times. He loves us. This is how we are to love our husbands. Love him when the situation is bad and it hurts to love him. Love him in the good times, and the bad times. Love him when he is down. Love him when he is confused, scared, or has lost his way. Love him when that's all you have. We don't always have to like them, but love is a must. It's not a cliché. Love can conquer all things.

2. _Joy._ The joy of the Lord is our strength. When your husband is acting like a different person, and not the man you fell in love with, don't lose your joy. When the bill collectors are call-

ing, and your house note is due, but you don't have the money, it's either buy food, or pay your mortgage; when your husband loses his job, or worse when he loses his way, and his faith is lacking, you have to protect your joy. When you have cried and can't cry anymore, and the hurt is nothing but a numb feeling because you are immune to it, the joy of the Lord is your strength. When you don't understand, can't feel, or hear God, the joy of the Lord is your strength. Count it all joy as you go through divers temptations because the Lord is with you. He will give you beauty for ashes and joy for your mourning. Don't look at the situation. Look at the joy. I'm not saying fake it until you make it, nor am I referring to being happy. Happiness is the result of happenstance. You may cry, but you can still have joy. You may not understand, but you can still have joy. Your marriage may be going through, or will go through some turbulent times, but look up because weeping may endure for a night, but joy comes in the morning.

3. _Peace._ And may the peace of God that surpasses all understanding keep you. Jesus said, _"Peace I give you and I leave with you, not as the world gives you,"_ John 14:27. In the midst of the storm, focus on the peace of God. He will keep you in perfect peace when your mind is stayed on Him. You need peace in the midnight hour. God's peace will keep you from losing your mind. Again, know when to fight your battle. Pick the battles that will cause the least harm or damage. Pete doesn't always pick up after himself. This used to make me angry, but he does a lot of other things around the house. Whenever there is a problem or something needs to be fixed, I never have to worry about it. He always fixes it or gets someone to fix it. The lawn is always beautifully maintained. He notices when I get a bruise

or scar on my body. And after all these years, he still makes me laugh. I can focus on and get upset about the things he doesn't do, or I can focus on the things he does that adds much to the marriage. It's easier to pick up the things or remind him in a joking manner, rather than argue about a pair of socks that I could've easily picked up. I choose peace instead of war.

4. _Longsuffering_. You will be challenged in marriage, and this is probably the hardest of all the Fruit. In this you will learn patience as you've never known. You will learn how to love in spite of how you feel. Be patient with him if he is not doing what he is supposed to do. That's when you need to pray for him. Be patient with him when he doesn't operate on your schedule, or your wish list. He isn't suppose to; he should operate on God's schedule. Remember, he is learning how to become the man God created him to be. It's a process. Sometimes, the process takes years. Be patient in the process. Your husband will get to his designated place at the appointed time.

5. _Gentleness (Kindness)._ It's funny, as women, we want our husbands to be gentle and thoughtful. We want them to be sensitive to our needs, concerns and our gender. We've forgotten about their needs and concerns. We forget that yes, they are men, but they are sensitive too. They have needs and desires, and surprisingly, they are not always intimate. They are not able to express themselves openly or as verbally as women, but men have moments too. We want them to treat us as queens, but we forget that they need to be treated as kings too, especially in their own home. Sometimes we have to encourage them with kind and gentle words, not harsh words. Yes, it's frustrating at times, but think of how your Father in heaven always deals with you, particularly in those moments when you are be-

ing hard-headed and stubborn. My mother would always say, "A hard head makes a soft behind, but soft words can cause the most obnoxious person to crumble." That is why we are called the salt of the earth. Salt produces flavor for a bland meal. Sometimes we have to produce the kind words to flavor our husband's disposition. Sometimes we need to give him a hug and let him know how much you appreciate him. Provide grace for him as Jesus does for you.

6. _Goodness_. I like what the Bible says as it pertains to this Fruit: "*Do unto others, as you want others to do unto you,*" Matthew 7:12. Treat others well, regardless of how they treat you. This includes your husband or your husband-to-be. As Christians, we are called to live Holy and righteously. Sometimes in this world this is a hard thing to live up to; but, we are not of this world. Being good should not be an act; but a way of life for us, for God is good and we are replicas of Him. No, I didn't say perfect, I said good. To be and do good to the best of our abilities is all God wants from us. Sometimes when your husband is being ill-tempered, fix him his favorite meal, or draw a bubble bath for him. Again, if you want your husband to treat you as a queen, treat him as a king.

7. _Faith (Faithfulness)_. "*Without faith it is impossible to please God,*" Hebrews 11:6. In marriage, you are going to need faith. You are going to need faith to maintain the ups and downs, the trials and tribulations, frustrations, disappointments, and even the marriage itself. It is easy to focus on the situation, the circumstances, the finances, the children, ministry, or work. All of these things can weigh a marriage down if we focus on them. The Word of God says, "*We walk by faith and not by sight,*" 2 Corinthians 5:7. It also says that the things we see are not what we

really see. In our marriages we must look unto Jesus, the Author and Finisher of our faith. In regard to faith, we must also be faithful in our marriage. Understanding we are two; it's not one anymore. You need to be faithful in your finances and in your role as a wife to your husband. You must be trustworthy and reliable. Remember, *"Faith is the substance of the things hoped for….,"* Hebrews 11:1.

8. _Meekness_. When we use the word meek, we associate it with a weak, passive or feeble person. In reality, a meek person is a strong person of character, integrity and humility. It is a person who doesn't have to prove her worth. She doesn't have to fight back when picked on. She allows the Lord to fight and win her battles. She has disciplined herself to learn to keep quiet. She knows what battle to fight and what battle to let go. In marriage, there will be many times when you have to display this Fruit. Let me forewarn you, this is not an easy fruit to display. Sometimes when your husband is off course, or keeps making the same mistakes, it is easy for us as women to tell him the right way to go, and not always with seasoned words. In these instances, you must allow the Lord to lead your husband. There are times when you have to appear weak, even though you're not. You are being meek, and this is pleasing to God. Always remember that God has your back; therefore, you don't have to be Super Woman or Wonder Woman. You just have to submit to the authority, and let God be God. By the way, Wonder Woman and Super Woman are cartoon characters.

9. _Temperance (Self-Control)_.). As Christians, everything must be done decently, in order and in moderation. This is where many of us need help, including me. Self- control or temperance denotes self-mastery in a thing. It includes the ability to

control impulses such as, shopping too much, eating too much, speaking too much, or in my case learning how to discipline yourself to keep quiet. As women today, if we are not careful, we can tear our husbands down with our words (regardless if they are true or not). Sometimes it takes a strong woman to be quiet. (The Lord is still working with me on this Fruit.)

I say this as I close. I've covered many relevant topics throughout this book as it pertains to a wife. However, If you don't grasp anything else, grasp this: Before you bring anything else to the marriage, bring God's Fruit of the Spirit. If you do, your marriage will be a blessing, and one to emulate.

Conclusion

"Are You Sure You Are Ready to Be a Wife"

It was late one night, and I couldn't sleep. I looked over at my husband. Nestled and sound asleep with the cover over his head, he looked so peaceful. Not wanting to disturb him, I went into the family room. Normally, I would read a book, or pray, but for some reason I turned on the television. I record a lot of shows on my DVR. When I get a chance I go back and watch them. I have almost six months of shows I still need to watch. On this particular night, I found myself not wanting to watch any of the shows I had recorded, so I began to surf the channels.

I came across a show I am ashamed to admit intrigued me so much that I found myself glued to the set. It didn't help that it was a marathon showing, and I sat and watched it from 12:30 am until 4:00 am. Was it good? I don't know, but I was fascinated by it that I couldn't turn it off. The funny thing is it's not the type of program I usually watch. I'm not a big fan of reality TV, drama, crime or mystery shows. I enjoy situation comedies and romance movies, preferably from the eighties, nineties, and the first part of this century. This particular show had me so engrossed that sleep was no longer a priority. It was disappointing when 4:00 am came, because I wanted to watch some more.

I don't know if I was led by the Holy Spirit to watch this show, but I believe I was. Don't shoot me down before hearing me. Remember I stated that I didn't know if the show was good. I wasn't looking at it from an entertainment perspective, but from a spiritual one. It had its moments. It made me smile. It even made me laugh. But, the truth is it made me think and see how twisted we have become. Not to give the plot away for copyright purposes, but it was about strong, successful women, who all had it going on, or living the "bling" life, as we call it today. In those short hours, there was plenty of drama, sex and alcohol. In almost all the scenes, they guzzled alcohol as if it was water. I believe each woman had two or more sexual partners. There was talk about getting mine, I don't need a man, I want a man, and I am the man. Like I stated, it was drama, drama and more drama.

In that short time span, the women encountered STDs, unwanted pregnancy, infidelity, blackmail and theft. In all of this, regardless of the crisis, the women dressed impeccably and glamorously. Did I fail to mention that they were all beautiful, with the perfect shape, face and body? And they also drove expensive cars, lived in beautiful homes, had successful careers, and enough money to satisfy their material needs. It was Hollywood at its best.

When the marathon was over, I turned off the television and sat thinking about what I had just witnessed. Stunned, I let out a long sigh and small laugh, and cried, "Lord, you want me to write this book when the enemy has glamorized sin to this magnitude. Women are not going to want to read a book about how to be a wife. They are going to look at the clothes, the cars, the money, the fabulous lifestyles, the great sex, the parties and want those things."

And this is where many of us are today. We want the "bling." We want the glamorous life that Hollywood and magazines portray. However, no matter how glamorous you try to make it, no matter how beautifully you dress it up; no matter how fun it looks, no matter how you masquerade it, sin is sin. Yes, the women appeared to have it going on. Yes, looking from the outside in, you want what they have. But at what cost? What price do you want to pay for it?

Hollywood's job is to sell you the illusion. They want you to buy into the fairy tale. Unfortunately, many of us have. We don't want to be wives. We want to be like the women we see in the magazines or on television. We want to be like Eve. We want the pretty fruit that will make us like God. We fail to comprehend that what we see is not what we really see. If we dig deep and see with our spiritual eyes, we will see the hurt and the pain. We will see the sin.

For the past twenty (+) years, I have been married to a wonderful, God-fearing man. A man. Not a super hero, not a god, not a perfect specimen, but a man. My love for him continues to grow, especially now that I know he is not my knight in shining armor. The more I see his imperfections, the more my love for him grows, the more I want to share his life with him. I want to share his trials, tribulations, his ups, his downs, his set-backs, his failures, his triumphs, and his successes. The more I see the man (my husband) the more I want to be his woman (his wife).

God is such a gentle, a compassionate, loving, kind, longsuffering, and merciful God; however, He is also a God of order. And in His order, He does not go against His Word. I think sometimes, as Christians, we forget this. I believe that our perspective of God is that He will allow us to do whatever we want to do without the consequences, if we always repent and ask for His forgiveness. That's how many of us see Him. We forget about His sovereignty. His wrath, or that He is God. I am not trying to scare or intimidate you into fear or manipulation. All I am trying to convey is that we sometimes forget that God is still God.

How does this relate to being a wife? Well, we have to understand how God views the wife and her role in the marriage. Before you say, "I do," go back to the scriptures and learn what they say about the wife's role. Seek guidance and wisdom from seasoned, matured Christian women who understand the role of a wife. More importantly, seek the Holy Spirit for your answers. What better person to give you the truth than The One who is Truth. Do not get married to get married, to have a warm body in your bed, or to have someone to take care of you. If you are getting married for any of those reasons, you are on your way to disaster.

Being a wife is a gift from God. With every gift, especially if it's an expensive one, we need to know how to appreciate it. God wants us to keep it, cherish it, and most of all cherish Him for giving it to us. God gave me a beautiful gift when he gave me Pete as my husband. His best gift is Jesus.

In regard to the television show, in spite of how successful each woman was, at the end of the day, when the show was over, they each said the same thing. They wanted a man. They didn't want to be a wife; they just wanted a man. Alas, they went home alone. They didn't have a man, and they won't because drama sells. It's good TV to make you tune in next week.

I pray that this book has ministered to you. I know it ministered to me.

Now again I ask you, "Are you sure you're ready to be a wife?"

If you are, congratulations and God bless you! Always keep Jesus first in your marriage. Now, let the journey begin.

Fannie

Works Cited

1. Ramsey, Glen, Strong's Concordance, Reference. Apple App Store. Version 2.0.1, November 2, 2013.

2. "Baggage." Def. 1. Pg. 38. *Merriam-Webster's New Dictionary of the English Language*. 2001. Print.

3. "Luggage." Def. 1. Pg. 309. *Merriam-Webster's New Dictionary of the English Language*. 2001. Print.

4. "Contain." Def. 1. Pg. 114. *Merriam-Webster's New Dictionary of the English Language*. 2001. Print.

CPSIA information can be obtained
at www.ICGtesting.com
Printed in the USA
FFOW02n1155200415
12741FF